Wellington

IN THE 1920S AND 1930S

ALLAN FROST

FONTHILL

Wellington Town War Memorial: The lych gate, erected in 1922 in the overgrown grounds of All Saints parish church, was regarded by many as a symbol of the futility of war and the blight cast by politicians upon the lives of ordinary citizens. Although not used as a lych gate in the accepted sense (i.e. coffins resting for a few moments before being transported along the path and into the church during funerals), the gate is the focal point for annual Services of Remembrance. Its inside walls contain tablets naming townsfolk who died in the two world wars.

For my sister Margaret, a child of these times.

First published 2013

Fonthill Media Limited
Millview House, Toadsmoor Road
Stroud, Gloucestershire
GL5 2TB

www.fonthillmedia.com

Copyright © Allan Frost, 2013

The right of Allan Frost to be identified as the Author of this work has been asserted in accordance with the Copyrights, Designs and Patents Act 1988.

ISBN 978-1-78155-261-2

British Library Cataloguing in Publication Data. A catalogue record for this book is available from the British Library.

Typeset in 10pt Sabon LT.
Typesetting and Origination by Fonthill Media.

Printed in Great Britain.

Contents

One of the 11th November Armistice Day Parades during which the King's Shropshire Light Infantry march from Church Street and past town dignitaries standing on a 'saluting base' rostrum erected outside the Wrekin Hotel in Market Square. The War Memorial lych gate is visible at top centre.

The Wellington Urban District Council office in Walker Street as it appeared in the 1930s. During the 1920s it was rather grandly called the Municipal Chambers, and 'Public Buildings' at other times.

Originally built as a meeting place by the Town Improvement Commissioners in 1883, it was the logical place for occupation by their successor body in 1894, Wellington Urban District Council (WUDC). The Council was dissolved in 1974 when Wrekin District Council assumed responsibility for the governance of Wellington and other towns in the area under local government reorganisation measures.

The town horse drawn fire engine was stored in one of the arched doorways until the 1920s; the bell in the belfry on the roof was rung to call volunteer firemen to duty, wherever they worked or lived, and whatever the time of day or night.

Staff of *Wellington Journal & Shrewsbury News* outside their premises between Church Street and Queen Street, 1935. 'The Journal', first issued in 1854, was published weekly and sold throughout Shropshire. It kept everyone on top of local news. From left to right: Charlie Lewis, Eric Wilson, Alf Walker, Tom Deakin, Jack Shorter, Frank Worsley, ? Owen, Les Treherne, Cliff Nicholas, Sammy Cotton. Fourth row: -?-, Stan Jones, -?-, George Brown, Horace Bagley, -?-, Bill Tidman, ? Musselwaite, Guy Hill, George Hickman, Charlie Roden. Third row: Sammy Steventon, ? Overton, Jack Churm, Fred Woolley, Alf ('Sankey') Painter, -?-, Harry Edwards, ? Perry, -?-, Arthur Clayton. Second row: -?-, Vera Dyer, George Leake, Harold Leake, Vic Leake, Charles Leake (proprietor, born 1854, died 1937), -?-, Joe Leake, Ethel Leake, -?-, -?-. Front row: Albert Bridgeman, ? Hickman, Jackie Scott, Bill Bishton, -?-, Reg Vaughan.

Introduction

Wellington's inhabitants experienced mixed fortunes during the period between the two world wars. It took several years for the devastating aftermath of the badly managed Great War of 1914-18 to be pushed to the back of everyone's minds, and even longer before a degree of economic stability was restored. Then, just as things were looking good and a golden age of reinvigorated commerce beckoned, townsfolk were plunged into the disruptive effects of yet another dreadful conflict.

It's human nature to view past times through rose tinted spectacles, believing them to be less fraught and considerably more satisfying than the conditions in which we live today. Photographs of the time seldom show litter-strewn streets or gaudy shop signs, an over-abundance of 'street furniture' or advertising signs positively shouting at passers-by, exhorting them to part with every penny of their hard-earned wages.

There are good reasons why this period in British (and Wellington's) history should be treated with some caution. It's all too easy to draw the wrong conclusions. Compared with the World War I period, the 1920s and '30s must have seemed golden in view of reigning peace, improving living conditions and, possibly for the first time for some folk, a little spare cash in the pocket. But not everyone was happy. Progress can seem exceedingly slow moving to those whose ways of life are well below those of their 'betters'.

The Twenties and Thirties presented a period of mixed fortunes for the inhabitants of Wellington. They can be regarded as an interval during which the traditional foundations of social structure underwent subtle change and the gap separating the living standards of the middling and lower classes was beginning to narrow. Nevertheless, despite some significant change in the economic role played by women during the Great War, a girl leaving school was still expected to take a position as a domestic servant in a well-to-do household or (until the day she got married) in a factory (like the Chad Valley Wrekin Toy Works in New Street) or some other industrial concern.

Economic progress in a variety of fields also had an impact on the way people lived, especially when it came to leisure pursuits and social interaction. Petrol-driven motor vehicles became a daily sight rather than a rare occurrence, for example. Visits to cinemas and theatres, and an evening spent dancing to live music became, for an increasing number of people, regular activities to ease the tensions of everyday existence.

After the trauma of one dreadful conflict came a time of adjustment, hope and raised expectations. It wouldn't last. All too soon, Wellingtons found themselves preparing for another uncompromising war.

A seemingly incessant flow of legislation requires local authorities to take action depending on what its Acts and recommendations dictate.

From 1930 onwards, in an effort to rein in poor driving habits by inconsiderate motorists and other road users, councils found themselves having to install directional signposts to make travel easier, and white painted road markings in certain places, like road junctions, to minimise accidents.

The Highway Code was first published in 1931. Local police and council workers were expected to ensure strict adherence to the law was observed by all road users, and prosecuting where it was deemed necessary.

Speeding and lack of consideration at junctions was just one area which needed attention. This council employee is getting to grips in 1933 with SLOW stencils and a seemingly small can of white paint.

George Harding, who died in 1950 and lived at 35 Park Street when this photograph was taken in the 1930s, was entrusted with driving the slow-moving steam roller – pride of the Wellington Urban District Council's maintenance department.

Chapter One

Civic Scene

Thanks to national government involvement, local councils were encouraged to raise their game by increasing property portfolios (euphemistically known these days as social housing), embarking on slum clearance projects, improving educational establishments and providing more in the way of welfare facilities. The interwar years seemed full of promise to town planners and local politicians.

Wellington Urban District Council (and not forgetting the Wellington Rural District Council based in Tan Bank) was not slow in embracing these opportunities and, like their subsequent successors, made a number of developmental blunders which would inevitably result in a loss in the cultural and historical character in the town.

The 1930s, for example, witnessed the beginning of a process of property acquisition with a view to demolition and replacement of housing blocks: in 1932, a demolition report centred on an area of High Street known as Little Ireland marked the start of a drawn-out scheme which wouldn't be completed until the 1970s.

The idea of purchasing the former vicarage at The Priory and its magnificent gardens with a view to turning them into a public park died when it became impossible to raise the money necessary to fund the scheme; instead, the land was sold to developers to build the large Roseway private housing estate. Permission was also granted for private dwellings to be erected in other locations, notably Herbert Avenue and Christine Avenue. Elsewhere, as along Slang Lane (renamed Hollies Road), council housing was expanded to accommodate folk turfed out from slums destined for demolition.

Not all council led schemes were ill considered. Some, like the 1932 construction of another reservoir near Buckatree Hall on Ercall Lane (occasionally still referred to as Wrekin Drive) was a major achievement and ensured a better supply of good quality drinking water for the town.

National legal requirements also led to a number of fundamental changes. Motoring laws in the early 1930s led to white painted road markings, experimental one way systems and, inevitably, driving lessons and licensing ... and an rise in the number of council employees required to cope with increasing involvement with public and public amenities, to the point where workmen were given their own steam roller to flatten tarmac on roads and in school playgrounds.

The council and other 'official' bodies did their utmost to improve both living standards and amenities, as will be evident throughout this book.

Not everything was tainted by gloom or doom.

Ex-RAF pilot Alan Cobham took these first aerial photographs of Wellington in 1922 for Aerofilms Ltd. This view looks south towards Christ Church (top centre) with King Street on the left.

The second 1922 photograph by Alan Cobham looks northwards along Tan Bank towards All Saints parish church, beyond the passenger railway station at right of top centre. Knighted in 1926, Cobham died, aged 79, in October 1973.

A Great War tank and field gun were donated to the town in 1920 in recognition of fundraising activities. It quietly rotted away in Bowring Recreation Ground until about 1937 when it was dismantled and sold for scrap to metal merchant James Rollason so that flower beds could be created.

Wellington Fire Brigade in Foundry Lane in the mid 1920s was led by Captain William Edwards who stands on the extreme left. Four of those on top of the horse drawn engine bought in 1909 are believed to be Rogers, Tudor, Hendy, Walker. Mr. Edwards was also an undertaker on Tan Bank. A new 'motor fire engine' was acquired from The Leyland Motors Ltd., of Leyland, Lancashire, in 1930.

'Bread and Dripping Lane' was the name given to Herbert Avenue, a new road of private houses begun in 1929 but which required comparatively high mortgages, which left little for life's necessities. One of Sidoli's stop-me-and-buy-one ice cream bicycles passes on the inside of a badly parked car.

Once home to the Lords Forester, Arlestone House as it appeared in 1935. Since known as Arleston Manor, there have been numerous alterations made to this late sixteenth century timber framed dwelling. Much of the surrounding Arleston Estate was sold to sitting tenants in 1918.

The Priory as it appeared in 1933. This Georgian building and the large estate which surrounded it, was the vicarage of All Saints parish church. It was all apparently gifted in the middle of the nineteenth century by local benefactor Thomas Campbell Eyton of Eyton Hall.

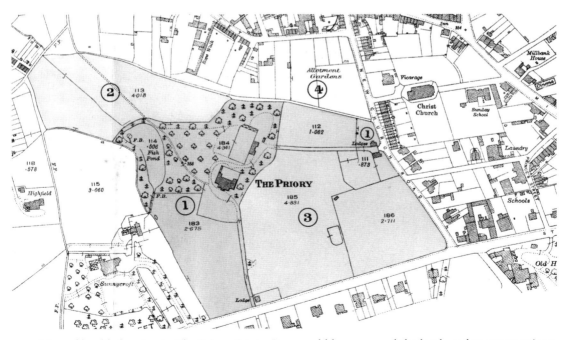

Map of land belonging to The Priory Estate. It was sold by 1937 and the land used to create private housing in Roseway, Rose Grove, Rosthwaite and Priory Road. Most houses were built by Fletcher Estates of Harlescott. The Priory itself, after serving as a nursing home, was demolished in 1962.

Robert Gwynne, founder of the firm which became Gwynne's Solicitors at Edgbaston House, Walker Street, examines documents relating to the National Savings scheme, 1937. As well as being Clerk to the Poor Law Guardians and Superintendent Registrar, he acted for many official bodies in the town.

Telegraph engineers travel from pole to pole with their handcart carrying a ladder and tools to perform essential maintenance, late 1920s. The Post Office was responsible for telephone and telegram services as well as letter and parcel deliveries.

There is some doubt about the date of this postcard photograph of uniformed delivery men standing with their bicycles outside the Church Street Post and Telegraph office. Although the postmark says 1921, it may well date from a few years earlier.

By 1929, when this photograph of staff was taken, the Post Office had relocated from Church Street to purpose built premises in Walker Street. Head Postmaster W. Hall is seated front row, cntre.In the row behind him are Bert Williams and Harry Bowles (respectively fourth and fifth from the left).

All Saints parish church, 1920s. Erected in 1790 to replace a medieval church severely damaged during the English Civil War, the church yard had become cluttered by (mainly) Victorian monuments and cast iron fenced family vaults, making it impossible to keep tidy.

The East Window area inside All Saints, decorated with what appears to be memorial wreaths as part of Remembrance Day services, 1920s. The interior of the church has seen many alterations since then. All eight bells were rehung in 1929; of them, five are dated 1713 and hung in the previous church.

CHRIST CHURCH, WELLINGTON.

Table of Fees.

BAPTISMS.

	£	s.	d.
Certificate of Baptism - - -			
at time of Baptism, 2s. 7d., later		3	7

MARRIAGES.

	£	s.	d.
Publication of Banns - - -		3	9
Certificate of Banns - - -		1	6
Marriage after Banns - - -		15	9
Certificate of Marriage, - - -			
at time of Marriage 2s. 7d., later		3	7
Marriage by Licence with Certificate	1	3	4
Marriage by Special Licence - -	1	11	6
Marriage: reduced fee for Labourers		11	3
No reduced fees on Sundays and Festivals.			

BURIALS.

	£	s.	d.
In Single Vaults (Vicar's Fee) -	1	6	0
Other Fees as for best Ground at Wellington Cemetery.			

January 1st, 1920.

J. P. ABBEY,
Vicar.

Christ Church, after which New Church Road is named, celebrated it centenary with floodlights in 1937. The Rev. James Phillips Abbey was its fifth and longest serving vicar, from 1913 to 1962. His Table of Fees for 1920 shows the maximum he was allowed to charge for common activities.

The Rev. Abbey (centre) and church members watch as the new Centenary Bell is manoeuvred into place in Christ Church tower. The bell weighs 2 tons 16lbs, is about 4 feet (120cms) high and 5 feet (150cms) in diameter. A service of thanksgiving and dedication took place in July 1939.

A joyful wedding group congregates outside St. Patrick's Roman Catholic church in the 1920s. The church, opened in August 1906, replaced an earlier one on Mill Bank whose roof had collapsed. The large crucifix by the front door was erected *c.*1920 as a memorial to the Fallen of the Great War.

New Street Methodist church with gates which were removed during the Second World War as part of the scrap for munitions campaign. The lane to the right led to Belmont Hall, a short-lived private school run by Captain Alfed Jason Froom from the late 1920s; it went bankrupt in 1932.

Methods of countering gas attacks were being practised as early as 1938 when war was likely to begin without warning. County Council roadmen form a volunteer decontamination squad on the Priory Estate as part of a series of County air raid lectures and survival drills.

Wellington Rural District Council offices in Tan Bank were used by members of the Women's Voluntary Service in 1939 to pack 18,000 Ration Cards for distribution to residential homes in preparation for belt-tightening measures when war began. From left to right: Miss Lovatt, Mrs. Lovatt, Miss Pearce, Miss Dale, Mrs. Ramsbotham, Mrs. Ritchie and Mrs. Hall. Similar distributions, with collection points and times advertised in *Wellington Journal*, followed as the conflict continued.

War preparations behind the police station in Church Street, 1939. Workmen fill hessian bags with sand and volunteer scouts stack them ready for distribution to yet-to-be-determined buildings whose protection during the impending war was considered essential.

Comrades together. Seen at Locking Camp, Weston Super Mare, August 1939 are (back row, left to right): Les Machin, -?-. Front: Bill Durrance, possibly Corporal Trinnick, Keith Axon. Even though he sports the King's Shropshire Light Infantry (KSLI) badge, Bill joined the Grenadier Guards.

Two sides to the same story: happy smiling faces of evacuee children from the Smethwick area pose for the camera soon after disembarking from trains at Wellington station in late August 1939. Local families were supposed to keep some 1,600 children safe for the duration of the war.

An impromptu, unposed photograph taken moments after the previous one in the same location. Young children wearing brown cardboard luggage tags in their lapels struggle to cope with heavy luggage and the misery of separation as they enter unknown territory. Not everyone stayed for long.

The narrow entrance into Market Square from New Street was the cause of numerous awkward situations for many decades, and probably more than a few centuries, especially when vehicles (whether horse drawn or motorised) were allowed to travel in both directions. Bollards and cast iron posts have been placed strategically at various times to protect vulnerable windows, not always successfully.

The timbered building on the left has accommodated several businesses throughout its long life, but the sole occupier during the interwar period was Walter Davies, gent's outfitter and clothier.

On the right is the sun blind protecting produce at A.L. Boyle's fruit shop, next to which is J.C. Lloyd's grocery store, and beyond that is Hilton & Sons boot dealers. Judging from town directories and examining this combination of shops in this location, the photograph dates to the mid 1930s.

Market Square, looking south, late 1920s. Walter Davies's gents' outfitter has pride of place in the old timber framed building, flanked on the left by Melias Colonial Stores on the corner of New and Crown Streets, and on the right by Boots the Chemist at the entrance to Duke Street.

Chapter Two

Street Scenes

One notable aspect when scrutinising old street views and comparing them with modern photographs is the remarkably minimal street furniture. This may be because plastic had yet to be invented, with the result that most commodities were wrapped in biodegradable brown paper or reusable bags made of leather, wicker or jute. Naturally, this meant far less work for Urban District Council street cleaners armed with brushes, dustpans and galvanised bins on wheels.

Furthermore, with the absence of man-made sheet materials, shop signs gave a subdued, more respectable appearance with painted background and hand-crafted writing. However, shaped lettering, fashioned from wood or Bakelite, became more common from the mid 1920s onwards, giving a prominent three-dimensional, ultra modern feel. Perhaps such attention-seeking signs, slightly out of kilter with the traditional standards of the day, have always marked the next stage of unrelenting progress which continues to this day.

It's always fascinating to compare other stages of economic and social progress in scenes captured by camera during consecutive decades. Horse-drawn carts and wagons were slowly giving way to petrol-driven motorised vehicles which were less demanding than their steam-powered, heavy-wheeled predecessors. Motor cars were still relatively rare during the 1920s but became more obvious in town centre streets as the 1930s progressed. Judging from the scenes shown here, one-way traffic systems had yet to be introduced and subsequently enforced, and the present day concept of pedestrianisation not yet an urban planner's dream.

Wellington's streets were virtually devoid of people on Sundays and Wednesday (early closing day) afternoons, and steadily busy at all other times except general market days (limited to Thursdays and Saturdays during this period) when shoppers from surrounding towns and villages flooded the streets with tidal waves of seething humanity in search of life's necessities and entertainment.

Mondays (the day upon which the town's housewives did their laundry and prayed for breezy, dry weather to enable them to get the ironing done before husbands returned from work) attracted members of the farming community. It was then that the weekly cattle market and periodic sheep and pig auctions took place at the Smithfield and country folk bought agricultural essentials (including machinery, seed, fertilisers and shotgun cartridges) as well as everyday items like clothing, household goods and exotic foodstuffs such as bananas and tinned oranges.

Market Square, looking northwards, late 1920s/early 1930s. Motor cars were becoming a more frequent phenomenon, juxtaposed with more common bicycles and traditional delivery basket-weave handcarts. The original 'Neale's The Stores' sign was about to be changed to 'Pearks Tea Stores'.

View from Market Square into Church Street, 1920s, with the Post Office directly on the bend. The Lych Gate was dedicated in 1922, and the horse trough (installed by plumber Thomas Newman), in the wall on the corner into Station Road, is surrounded by an inscription for the town baths.

Church Street, early 1920s. Soon, the Post Office premises would be occupied by Agnew's tailor's shop. Next door, John Jones's stationery and printing works supplied a wide range of writing accoutrements and accurate town directories. The *Wellington Journal* office was next door to Jones's.

Compare this 1930 scene with the one above. D.W. Agnew has replaced the Post Office and R. Partridge's newsagent's occupies Jones's former premises. The *Wellington Journal* office remains but on the right, the National Westminster Bank has replaced all the old property on The Green.

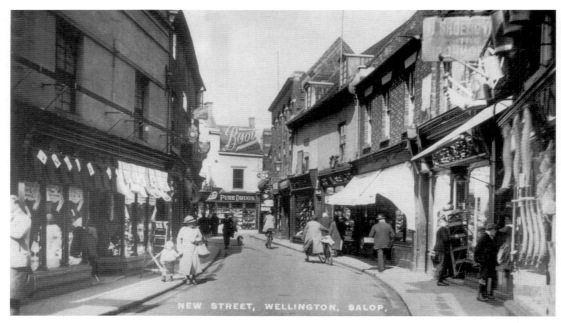

Western New Street, 1920s, dating from the thirteenth century. It comprised narrow shops; many had been built on long plots of ground which, since medieval times, had accommodated outbuildings, workshops and gardens. Shopkeepers and their families usually lived above and behind their shop.

Central New Street also in the 1920s. The man walking away on the right, wearing a seaman's cap, is chimney sweep 'Sooty' Adams. Behind the two men on the extreme right is Sidoli's restaurant, opened by Artura Sidoli, who was the first person to import espresso machines into Britain.

A little further east along New Street, early 1930s. Note the blinds considered necessary to protect goods in shop windows against discolouring. Traffic was two-way at the time. Note the gas street lamps, lit and unlit every night and day by a bicycle-riding man wielding a hook on a long pole.

Madame Davie's 'wardrobe' dealership sold second hand clothes at 2 High Street in the early 1930s before moving over the road by 1937 to number 19, whereupon number 2 became Agnes Harvey's grocery shop. The Chad Valley Wrekin Toy Works with its iron fence (removed before the start of the Second World War) lies in New Street three doors from the open gates to Noah Frost's bakery yard.

High Street began at Chapel Lane on the left and was created during the 1870s when New Street was split into two. The bunting across the road was in celebration of King George V's Silver Jubilee in May 1935. High Street was almost like a separate village, with many small shops and inns.

View eastwards along Haygate Road with All Saints parish church visible in the far distance. Harry Bowdler's West End Stores grocery shop is on the left at number 48 next to the turning into Mansell Road. The shop was later run by Mr. Whiteley, previously of the Avenue Stores in Victoria Avenue.

The promise of traffic tail backs at the notorious Cock Hotel crossroads on the A5 was, in the late 1920s, an unlikely prospect. A patrolman controls what few vehicles there are. The appearance and subsequent proliferation of 'finger' signposts is almost entirely due to increasing motorised transport.

In 1937, the local council thought it best to install a traffic island at the Cock Hotel crossroads as a full time patrolman on points duty was inefficient. Further bottleneck build-ups ensued, with the result that the island was removed and replaced by more effective traffic lights in 1958.

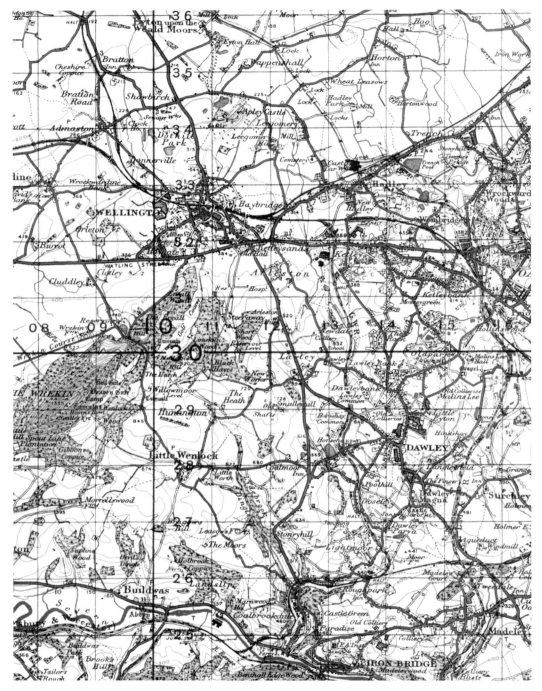

Ordnance Survey One Inch to the Mile map, mid 1930s. Wellington remained the prime centre for commerce and entertainment for people from the many towns and villages located between mining, manufacturing and agricultural locations. The Wrekin Hill continues to dominate the skyline.

Chapter Three

Transport and Industry

It is often the case that growth and prosperity are linked to improvements and developments in methods of transport. By 1920, railway services, for both passengers and the conveyance of goods (including livestock destined for Smithfield auctions) were well advanced and the contribution to supporting the local and wider economies was fully understood, which is one reason why long standing drainage problems at the passenger station were given priority treatment to rectify them.

However, new forms of transport were attaining an irreversible position of importance: petrol driven vehicles would, over the next two decades, replace traditional horse drawn carts. Garages became more numerous and facilitated the distribution of petrol; locally made or assembled motorised carriages, each with their own quirks and qualities, gave way to dealerships selling mass produced vehicles made in other parts of the country. Whereas rail enabled economic long distance delivery of heavy and bulky goods to depots and people to passenger stations in many towns and villages, lorries and buses were essential in those all-important final stages of journeys which could not be served by rail.

Gradually and inexorably, horses became less of a common sight on Wellington's streets, apart from the few required to make domestic coal deliveries; they would survive until the late 1950s. Among the earliest 'public transport' vehicles on roads were horse drawn charabancs (often converted carts fitted with bench seats and collapsible roof); these, too, were replaced by purpose built omnibuses in the 1920s which became an essential amenity within ten years. The cheapest form of transport for most people was the bicycle; the town was well served by established assemblers (like Perry's) as well as, increasingly, upcoming high street stores like Currys which sold mass produced bikes as well as toys and radios.

On the industrial front, Wellington would continue to prosper from a variety of manufacturers but, by 1939, many were on the verge of collapse as proprietors retired and markets dwindled in favour of imported products. Nevertheless, agricultural machinery and equipment, timber processing and wooden goods (such as furniture, household utensils and coffins) continued to thrive. Toy production took off in a big way when the Chad Valley Toy Works in New Street became established and designer Norah Wellings opened her Victoria Toy Works in King Street.

Against all odds, Wellington's industries managed to ride the troubled waters of the 1926 General Strike and the worldwide economic crash of the early 1930s.

Ryde House at 25 Walker Street was owned by Arthur Sockett who had used the premises for a variety of purposes. It had been a temperance hotel, an apartment and boarding house, a Registry Office for Servants, a 'general family and provision business' (a grocery shop) and, as seen here, for saddle and harness manufacturing.

Furthermore, the building had been the Coach & Horses public house from at least the 1870s until around 1916 when it closed, apparently a victim of restrictive 'DORA', the Defence of the Realm Acts, which led to the demise of many small hostelries.

Arthur Sockett acquired the property during the 1920s and continued until he was obliged to retire through ill health in 1939.

Samuel Perry started the cycle business up at Park Street around 1908 where he lived with his wife Mary Ann; they had fourteen children. Prior to moving to Park Street, he had been engaged in making bicycles in other locations around the town.

Samuel's son William ('Bill') Henry Perry, seen on the right in this 1930s photograph, took over the business about ten years before his father died in December 1939.

Born in 1908, Bill married Agnes Marston in 1938 and remained in Park Street where they brought up their three daughters: Janet, Mary and Dorothy. Janet took over the business about 1979. Bill, a well liked and respected businessman in the town for many years, died in May 1981.

In the early days, firms like Perry's bought component parts for bicycles from various manufacturers and assembled them on their own premises, adding bespoke parts to meet specific client requirements.

Bill frequently repaired inner tube punctures and adjusted worn brake pads, often at little or no charge.

Periodic flooding of tracks within the area occupied by the passenger railway station, probably due to an ancient stream passing through the centre of town not being adequately conduited, led to major disruption to all rail services between 1923 and (mainly) 1925 while remedial work was carried out.

Remedial work along the western section of railway track towards Bridge Road under way in 1925. Shunter engines and carriages were used to bring materials and remove debris, under instruction from Mr. G.H. Connor, Wellington Urban District Council's engineer and surveyor.

A steam engine passes westwards in the 1920s between the 'up' and 'down' platforms at Wellington railway station on a track reserved for non-stop through traffic and short-distance 'shunters'.

The Midland Red Omnibus Company of Birmingham's garage on Charlton Street opened in July 1932, after originally renting a garage owned by Wellington Transport Company in Mansell Road from July 1926. From an initial three vehicles, the fleet grew to 40 by the 1960s.

FORM P.S.V. 30/2/D

LICENCE No. **D** 01920

BADGE No **DD** 3798

ROAD TRAFFIC ACTS, 1930 to 1934.
LICENCE TO DRIVE A PUBLIC SERVICE VEHICLE.

THIS LICENCE is issued by the TRAFFIC COMMISSIONERS for the WEST MIDLAND TRAFFIC AREA and authories—

> John Jervis,
> 43, High Street,
> Wellington
> Shropshire.

Strike out the words which follow if not appropriate. to drive a public service vehicle of the type or types shown in the schedule below. This licence shall have effect as from 24th August 1935 and shall continue in force until 23rd August 1936.

Date of issue 17th August 1935

Fee 2/-

Signature of licensee (see Note 1) John Jervis

SCHEDULE.

Type or types of public service vehicles which the licensee is licensed to drive.

Any Single-decked Vehicle

Having come under pressure for better road safety, National Government embarked on a series of measures designed to improve standards of motoring (and raise a little extra money in the process). Coach operators required PSV licences to comply with the terms of Road Traffic Acts.

A unique (albeit slightly double exposed) photograph of John Jervis's first omnibus taken in the early 1930s when he was about to relocate his business to Wellington.

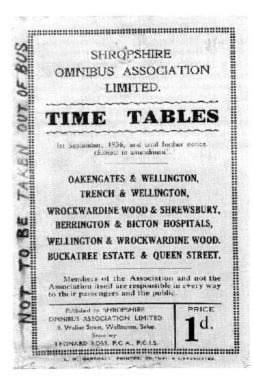

SHROPSHIRE
OMNIBUS ASSOCIATION
LIMITED.

TIME TABLES

1st September, 1936, and until further notice.
(Subject to amendment)

OAKENGATES & WELLINGTON,
TRENCH & WELLINGTON,
WROCKWARDINE WOOD & SHREWSBURY,
BERRINGTON & BICTON HOSPITALS,
WELLINGTON & WROCKWARDINE WOOD.
BUCKATREE ESTATE & QUEEN STREET.

Members of the Association and not the
Association itself are responsible in every way
to their passengers and the public.

Published by SHROPSHIRE
OMNIBUS ASSOCIATION LIMITED.
3, Walker Street, Wellington, Salop.
Secretary
LEONARD ROSS, F.C.A., F.C.I.S.

PRICE
1d.

L. W. MARSHALL, PRINTER, SQUARE, OAKENGATES.

Shropshire Omnibus Association was a collective of privately owned coach proprietors, originally formed during the 1920s as the Oakengates & District Small Bus Association, to look after their commercial interests. The Association published its own time tables (left) of services from Wellington to outlying towns and villages.

Earlier return-journey 'tickets' took the form of octagonal copper tokens (above), each bearing a number or letter allocated to each operator, which could be used on any service. A monthly 'reckoning' took place to distribute fare takings according to the proportion of tokens each operator had sold. The system was cumbersome and led to arguments, so paper tickets were adopted.

Telephone : 46
Telegrams : "Ensor, Wellington, Salop."
—
C. A. ENSOR
Sole District Agent for
AUSTIN, CLYNO, ROVER,
LEA-FRANCIS & VULCAN
CARS.

Open and Closed Cars for Hire

Exchanges Transacted. Special
Attention to Tuition and After
Service.

A good selection of Second-hand
Cars always in Stock

☞ **Lock-up Garages to Let**
—
The GARAGE, BRIDGE ROAD
WELLINGTON   -   SALOP

Established 1864.   Telephone 132.
CLIFT & SON (DUNCAN CAMPBELL, Proprietor.)
Excelsior Motor and Carriage Works,
WELLINGTON, SALOP.

Speciality : Light, Strong, Elegant Motor and Carriage Bodies.
Re-Painting and Upholstering to all kinds of Vehicles.
Rubber Tyres fixed at the shortest notice.

R. BERESFORD,
Motor & Cycle Stores.

Agent for HUMBER, CENTAURS, RUDGE-
WHITWORTH, FRANCIS, MONOPOLE,
RAMBLER, &c.   Repairs by Skilled Work-
men.   Cycles Built to Order; B.S.A. Fittings.
Accessories of all kinds.   Electric Lamps and
Batteries. Cycles for Hire at reasonable charges.

Note Address :
10, New Street, Wellington,
SALOP.

Telegrams : "Wingles, Wellington (Salop)."

THE
Wrekin Motor Co.
Motor Engineers
and Agents.

LARGE GARAGE FOR CARS.

Tyre and Petrol Stock. Repairs by a
Competent Staff of Skilled Mechanics.
Any well-known make of Car supplied.

Garage and Works:
Foundry Lane, WELLINGTON,
SALOP.

The transition from horse drawn to combustion engine powered vehicles led to the formation of new businesses like those of Charles Ensor and The Wrekin Motor Co. (the latter occupying premises previously used by E.P. Smith & Co., Agricultural Engineers), as well as Beresford's car and motorcycle parts shop (which also repaired prams). Others, like Clift & Son, ceased making traps, landaus and similar horse drawn vehicles and sold the goodwill and trading name to motor manufacturuers.

Reade's Garage on Watling Street opened around 1920, catering for 'passing through' traffic as well as a growing number of local drivers. From left to right: Ernie Evans, Herbert Cecil Reade (owner), Tom Manning, RAC patrolman (Ernie Dyas?), Charlie Goode and Alex Wright.

Shaw's Garage on Church Street may have dealt in motor cycles before Edward John Shaw (previously in partnership with Charles Ensor at Bridge Road) took it over, c.1920 and expanded facilities to include car sales, repairs and petrol filling. The workshop had a J.W. Clift roller shutter door. In 1935 the premises were acquired by the Waverley Garage which already had a garage in King Street.

PARK STREET GARAGE

(J. F. FERRIDAY)
WELLINGTON, SHROPSHIRE

ESTABLISHED 1919.   'Phone WELLINGTON 138.

For Cars, Motor Cycles

Motor Accessories. Repairs

by Competent Mechanics.

Wireless,

Electrical Goods.

Accumulators Charged.

**Satisfaction
Guaranteed.**

Recognising the demand for motor mechanics as more folk took up driving, small garages like that run by Joseph F. Ferriday in Park Street. It managed to survive until the late 1950s when it was acquired by Bill Doran and Matt Wright.

Ercall Garage, located below the Assembly Rooms of and in the former stable yard to the Ercall Hotel, Market Street, was in business from the late 1920s until the 1980s. The men seen here with new Austin Six cars in the 1930s are believed to be proprietor P. Pierce and David Church.

Memorabilia from Wellington's agricultural engineering firms. Bromley's traded in Bridge Road; W. Corbett in Alexandra Road; E.P.Smith in Foundry Lane and S. Corbett & Son in Park Street.

An example of a 1920s agricultural contraption: a seed sowing device intended to be pulled by horses across ploughed fields. This one was made by E.P. Smith & Co., at their Foundry Lane agricultural engineering factory. The business appears to have had a short life, ceasing around 1920.

This Wrekin model WR8 Root Cutter was manufactured by James Clay (Wellington) Ltd., whose Wrekin Foundry operated in Foundry Lane from the early 1900s). In addition to hand operated, time saving devices such as this, the company made other implements, including parts (like metal seats) for tractors. Production shifted to the Ketley Brook area in 1924.

Samual Corbett & Son's patented 'Plymouth' Royal First Prize Grinding Mill was one of their many award winning agricultural devices. They were sold throughout the world as well as within the United Kingdom. Nowadays they are considered museum exhibits but a few are apparently still in use.

Heating water, warming houses and acting as a stove for cooking were basic necessities in many domestic dwellings. Cast iron 'ranges', as they were called, met those needs.

Although Wellington had several businesses capable of casting iron into various shapes, none seems to have had the ability or urge to create its own range. Nevertheless, examples still exist bearing the names of town-based engineering firms, such as W. Corbett and Walter Davies, implying that their ranges were made in Wellington. They weren't.

Without exception, ranges carrying names with popular appeal, like 'Wellington' and 'Wrekin' were actually made for these firms by, for example, the Coalbrookdale Company and Sinclairs at Ketley, who supplied all the required parts in kit form.

All the Wellington firms had to do was carry out whatever structural work was necessary to accommodate a particular range from their catalogue ... and assemble it.

Thomas G. Newman's business on The Green at 8 Church Street began around 1890. With an expansion in the number of business premises and domestic dwellings in the town from the end of the nineteenth century onwards, opportunities for decorators also grew.

Customer requirements, however, encouraged the business to expand into other areas, like plumbing, central heating and, perhaps the most appreciated, sanitary work entailing indoor flushing toilets (as opposed to down-the-garden chemical closet privvies requiring regular emptying by the 'night soil man'). Newman's, in common with other firms engaged in similar activities, adapted to meet changing needs and expectations, which enabled it to compete and survive.

George York's business in New Street claimed to have been established in 1803. This 1937 advertisement expounds the virtues of its water supply, filtration and artesian well boring activities but it was previously well known and respected for the quality of its plumbing, heating, lighting and decorating services.

Artesian wells in and around Wellington were relatively numerous owing to the fact that much of the surrounding land comprises significant sand deposits.

However, founder William York was a baker here in 1821. By 1844, William had turned to selling ale at the George & Dragon inn, a few doors away, while his daughter Mary continued the baking trade until the 1870s.

The plumbing and glazing business seems to have begun between 1844 and 1851 after which William Henry York, William's son, took over. The George & Dragon closed and the premises were used solely for engineering, plumbing, etc., until the firm closed in the 1960s.

Thomas Wellings, a plasterer specialising in decorative as well as 'plain' plastering, had a workshop behind houses at the western end of Victoria Avenue. His daughter, Norah, would become internationally famous for her exquisitely made dolls.

There have been many high quality furniture manufacturers in Wellington but none was so renowned for church, school and office furniture as Henry Addison's, whose Waterloo Works were situated off Orleton Lane.

The 1929 Kelly *Directory of Shropshire* advertises the firm as, 'Inventors, patentees & manufacturers', whose designs for, among other products, tilting 'reversible' benches were essential equipment where seated adults or children facing in one direction in a meeting room might need to turn round to face the opposite direction without interrupting proceedings any more than necessary.

School class rooms were similarly supplied with cast iron framed double-seater oak desks with sloping lids complete with pen or pencil groove and sliding brass covered 'Welsh hat' inkwells.

The range of products continued to expand, as did the market for their products, some of which were bespoke orders for establishments of great importance where design and visual impact were as important as the quality.

Henry Addison & Co., Ltd., stopped trading at the end of the 1930s.

Henry Addison & Co., Ltd.

Telegrams: Addison's, Wellington, Salop | WATERLOO WORKS, WELLINGTON, SALOP. | Telephone: Wellington, Salop, 41.

Manufacturers of Church, School, College, Mission Room, Office and Library Furniture.

No. 182.

Hall Seating.

Also made with reversible back, and cheaper type with iron standards, also Convertible Table & Seat with iron standards. FOLDING PORTABLE TIP-UP CHAIRS.

Communion and Chancel Chairs and Furniture, also other interior woodwork for Churches, Chapels, Institutes, etc.

Panelling and other high-class Joinery Work.

FOLDING PARTITIONS FOR ALL PURPOSES.

ENQUIRIES SOLICITED.
DESIGNS & ESTIMATES FREE.

The acquisition of lorries to replace horse-drawn brewers' drays in 1929 enabled the Wrekin Brewery in Market Street to supply public houses over a much wider area, even to the Welsh coast. It was at this time that the firm began its remarkable rise to become what many believe was the largest privately owned brewery in the country, with over 200 pubs in its portfolio.

Wellington had always served the farming community which surrounded it by providing markets for their products as well as sourcing machinery, fertilisers and any number of farm-related items. Steeraway Farm off Lime Kiln Lane was one, owned in the 1920s by John Cetti.

Dothill Estate, 1923, with Dothill Park behind the horses and the dovecote and Dothill Farm to the right. Herbert Lewis guides the horses, presumably administering a form of crop care. The Lewis family lived in a tied cottage on the Dothill Estate for several decades. The last member of the Groom timber merchanting family to live here was Ernest, who died in 1944.

Wellington Smithfield, Bridge Road, *c.*1930s. These premises were created by Wellington Markets Company when their current Market Hall in Market Street was built in the 1860s. Barbers auctioneers acquired them in the early 1950s. Economic factors caused it to closed in January 1989.

View inside the Town Hall, Market Street, during an annual Wool Sale with Arthur Barber as auctioneer. His father John founded the firm, which still exists, in 1848. To supplement livestock auctions, wool sales began in 1860; fleece viewing took place in marquees in a field on Spring Hill or, occasionally, in the Market Hall. The last wool sale took place around 1940. The screen confirms the Town Hall's use as a cinema.

Arleston-born Norah Wellings 1893-1975) began her career as a designer at the Chad Valley Wrekin Toy Works until 1926 when she decided to form her own doll making business which was featured in this stand at the 1927 British International Fair ('The Big BIF').

In 1929 she moved into her own factory in the former Baptist chapel in King Street and expanded it several times to cope with demand.

Throughout her life, Norah was guided and supported by her brother Leonard. The factory closed soon after his death in 1959.

Her dolls were manufactured specifically for sale in luxury, high-quality stores like Harrods, Hamleys and Liberty, and abroad for Macy's and Bloomingdale's, and even one store in Cairo. Countless sailor dolls were made for cruise liners during the 1930s.

Norah puts the finishing touches to a head which would form the mould for numerous other dolls which, after expert workmanship by her employees, would be coiffed, dressed and packaged for the luxury toy market. A similar doll (of the *Cora* design) was presented to Queen Mary in 1927.

Chapter Four

Shopkeepers and Artisans

The 1930 *Directory of Wellington* by John Jones & Son states, 'The retail establishments cast no discredit upon a town of larger size, the traders study carefully the requirements of their customers, and residents who imagine they can shop to a greater advantage in larger centres of population will place themselves to great inconvenience and considerable expense, and fail to attain their object.' In short, Wellington's shop keepers provided an unbeatable service second to none.

The inter-war years was an era in which the streets in the town centre were characterised by thriving small businesses. The local economy depended on them, although the relative success of each enterprise should be viewed in the context of the time. Living costs were, by and large, stable. Profits were relatively small: sufficient to feed, clothe and accommodate a large family but hardly enough to raise standards of living to unusual heights. Reputation was everything to anyone in business, and unjustified increases in prices could easily encourage customers to go elsewhere; there were plenty of other shops offering alternatives.

Many families still lived in rooms behind and above their shop, an aspect of Wellington life which encouraged a greater degree of pride in the town's appearance than has been witnessed in recent years. Living on the premises provided its own highly effective 'neighbourhood watch' scheme.

These small businesses didn't just keep an eye on their property specifically and the town generally, they also looked out for each other, especially in such economically uncertain times. There was enough trade to enable everyone to make a decent living, so helping one's competitors was not a problem. For example, the author's grandfather, Noah Frost, who ran the family bakery and grocery store in (what was then part of) New Street helped other bakers in the town (Heath's, Jefferies' and Wheeler's) when they had credit difficulties in obtaining flour and other essential ingredients.

Other features which are no longer evident but were commonplace in this period are sun blinds above shop frontages. They protected shoppers and passers-by from both rain and sunshine as well as the stock enticingly displayed behind the window glass. During evenings and early closing days as well as on Sundays, these overhead blinds were furled into storage boxes above the window frames, and the window displays themselves were protected behind see-through sepia-tinted cellulose blinds or hidden by rolled-down fabric which could feature a printed advertisement but was more likely to be plain material.

Clothes maketh man ... and woman. Wellington had been blessed with numerous stores specialising in all things tailoring since the eighteenth century. Fred Bean at 25 New Street was a gents' outfitter who specialised in hats and hosiery.

TAILORED SUITS
FOR GENTLEMEN

Cut, Made and Finished in our own workshops from the best quality Cloths.

Scotch and Irish Homespuns, Cheviots, Saxonies and Worsteds from 5gns.

SERVICE : We offer Twelve Months Free Valeting Service with every Suit costing from 5½gns.   May we send you patterns ?

D. W. AGNEW,
Church Street   :   :   Wellington
Phone 125.

As tailors went, Agnews in Church Street was a relative newcomer whose shop had relocated from 4 and 6 St. John Street in the 1920s. It was still in business here over 40 years later.

Women were also well catered for when it came to the number of shops specialising in female attire. Not everything sold by Stephenson's at 43 New Street was made on the premises; by the 1920s, greater emphasis was being placed on 'buying in' stock, which helped keep at the forefront of fashion.

This photograph gives a rare 'women only' view inside J.L & E.T. Morgan's linen drapers, silk mercers, haberdashers, milliners, dress makers and ladies' outfitter shop at 3 Church Street, in the early 1920s. It was succeeded by Jackson's hat, boot and shoe dealership in 1928.

B.W. Rumins, 'The New Street Drapers' was how the firm described itself in the caption for this photograph from *John Jones's Directory of Wellington*, 1930. By 1939 the shop had been taken over by Bowens Ltd., also drapers.

Bata Shoe Organisation opened a store in New Street in the late 1930s, when its slippers were a marketing success at Christmas 1939. The company originated in 1894 at Zlin (now in the Czech Republic). It was its policy of selling cut price shoes which made it such a success for many decades.

Craddocks Bros Ltd. shoe store opened at 11 New Street in the late 1920s; this photograph probably dates to 1930. Frank Burton's chemist's shop had just opened in Thomas Shaw's former jeweller's. The window on the right was A.J. Arthur's baker's, soon to be part of F. W. Woolworth's new store.

John ('Jack') Henry Twinney had been trained as a surgical boot and shoe maker in Birmingham before opening his shop at 105 High Street. This photograph was probably taken around 1930 at this address but, owing to renumbering of High Street properties, it had become 97 High Street by 1937.

Alfred Barlow is thought to be the first ladies' hairdresser to set up business in Wellington. Advertisements for the firm made a point of emphasising that he had come to 40 New Street from Harrods in London in October 1911. It was not unusual for businessmen to claim previous experience at well known and respected establishments, but in Alfred's case it was true.

Until around 1929, Alfred and his family lived above the shop but, owing to a growth in sales of ground floor products, he decided to move into 40 Herbert Avenue. The hairdressing salons relocated upstairs at the shop, allowing the area for downstairs sales to be expanded.

Like other barber shops, Barlow's repaired umbrellas – it was a way of ensuring employees (of which there were twelve in the 1930s) had something to do during slack periods.

The shop was sold by Alfred's son Ronald in 1962.

Barlow's double fronted shop sold cosmetics (prefume was sold 'loose' before 1939) and toys in the front part of the store. Initially, its men's and ladies' hairdressing salons were at the rear but later relocated upstairs.

One of the hairdressing businesses to survive for well about a century was that begun by Frederick Richards at 6 Church Street, on The Green, in 1868. He died in 1910, whereupon his son Bert bought it from his mother Ann. Initially catering solely for men, opening hours were from 8am to 9pm; the reason for opening so early was that businessmen came for a shave on their way to work.

As the business outgrew its premises, Bert moved to 9 Market Square (aside) in 1920 where he was able to enlarge the range of tobacco and 'personal hygiene' products for sale, and expand into ladies hairdressing with all the latest salon equipment. Opening hours changed to 8.30am to 7pm, reflecting changes to shop opening times generally.

Some clients, like Sir Thomas Meyrick of Apley Castle, expected 'home visits', as did Wrekin College boys who benefitted from a contract for regular clipping.

The site of these shops in Market Square is now occupied by a closed W. H. Smith store which was built originally as a John Menzies stationery and book store. Brittain's was a grocery shop with a 'Model Bakery' on Haygate Road; it was sold to Morris's of Shrewsbury in 1943. Noblett's confectionery shop was, until the 1840s, the Six Bells inn, named after the number of bells in the old parish church.

Ben Robertson outside his 71 High Street hairdresser's in the 1930s. Bill was born in 1912 and took over the business from Benjamin Robinson. He lost the business in 1939 when he was called up to serve in the Army (the highlight of which was meeting King Olaf of Norway).

As with other local butchers, Franl Onions (standing in the doorway to his shop at 30 New Street) made sure customers knew he despatched his livestock humanely, including this Champion Beast acquired at the highly-competitive Smithfield Christmas Livestock auction.

OWEN, PORK BUTCHER

HAM & BACON CURER.

TRY OUR NOTED PORK SAUSAGE.

SPECIALITY:
Home-Made Pork Pies.

109 HIGH STREET, & MARKET HALL,
WELLINGTON.

Second only to Espleys' in reputation as trusted pork butcher's, Owen's took over a grocery-cum-bakery from a Mr. Bennett around 1913. Owen's subsequently concentrated on pork products and had a stall in Market Hall as well as the High Street shop.which also served as a slaughterhouse.

The problem with laying personalised mosaic tiles in the doorway to a shop means that it remains on view, as if to confuse would-be shoppers. J.W. Owen's shop at 4 Duke Street went out of business in 1909 yet it continued to advertise itself after McClure Bros., tailors and drapers, succeeded it.

Members of the Espley family had a long-standing reputation as pork butchers; the inter-war period could be regarded as their most significant, with branches spread throughout Shropshire and North Wales. They made a point of emphasising humane slaughter and professional standards of cleanliness.

The reputation of butchers and their products were things which had to be earned ... and maintained. Joseph Thomas Drury's establishment at 3, Market Street gave excellent service to customers from its beginnings in the early 1900s to its closure in the late 1930s.

John Alfred Smith, the proprietor of Smith's Fish Stores at 51 (since renumbered to 65) New Street takes a break with his wife and pet dog in the Medieval burgage-style long and narrow plot behind the shop premises, 1920s.

John took over the business from Thomas Palmer sometime between 1906 and 1913. The shop had been home to fruiterers and fishmongers, and licensed dealers in game, for around 100 years by the time Mr. Smith's daughter Nora Machin closed it down in 1960.

It then became the town's first Chinese restaurant, the Hung Hing and is currently occupied by Golden Scissors hairdressers.

Staff of Maypole Dairy Co. Ltd., outside their premises at 3 New Street, 1938. From left to right: Bob George, Dorothy Edwards, Irene Felton, Betty Hollis and Harry Griffiths (manager). Staff were noted for their ability to pat butter and wrap products in an expertly folded sheet of paper.

Pearks Stores or, more correctly, Peark's Dairies Ltd. at 15a Market Square was a well-frequented tea dealer's and grocery shop.

Unlike other small businesses during the inter-war years, this firm appears to have had a relatively short existence. It is mentioned in trade directories during the 1920s and 1930s but seems to have ceased trading by 1941.

Next door to Henry Baxter's drapery, 'Importer of High Class Provisions' was displayed prominently over the windows to J.C. Lloyd's shop in Market Square, *c.*1928. Staff were, from left to right: Roland Taylor, -?-, Jack Williams, Dorothy Owen, Margaret Tudor, Ruth Howells, Annie Davies, Harry Worgan, Margery Mason, George Mason (who later ran his own shop), Frank Lowe and Joe Vickers.

Wellington boasted many small family-run businesses. Clockwise, from bottom left: Noah and Mary Jane Frost take tea in their renowned bakery at 92 New Street, 1935; grocer Frank Tinsley at 61 High Street in the 1920s was famed for his home made ice cream; Tom Titley stands outside his father Herbert James Titley's Idol Cycle Works, 16 Walker Street, 1930s; Thomas Smith (photographed in the 1920s with his wife Ellen and sons (from left to right) Alfred, Vernon, George, Harold and daughter Marjory Ellen), ran a successful brush making shop at 47 (later renumbered 43) High Street.

Bates and Hunt's shop in Market Square (there was another in New Street), 1920s. The firm was the main pharmacy in Wellington for many years. Founded around 1850 by James Bates, the business was renamed when Joshua Hunt became a partner.

In the absence of televisions and similar distractions, many people looked to music for their entertainment. Field's shop in Station Road, now incorporated into HSBC Bank premises, was well ahead of the game when it came to practical as well as pre-recorded musical offerings.

Orleton Terrace lies between Mansell Road (probably named after a nineteenth century foundry owner in the town) and Slang Lane (the original name of what became Hollies Road, which took its name from one of Wellington's medical practitioners, Dr. G. Hollies).

Robert James ('Jim') Bishop had a small shop at number 17 in which he not only acted as a dealer in increasingly popular wireless radios but also as a grocer, stocking everything from Rinso washing powder to Lyons and Edglets Tea.

Besides being a shopkeeper from the 1930s, Jim was also responsible for maintaining the beacon on The Wrekin Hill during the 1940s and '60s.

J. T. COTTON,

(Late D Shoebotham)

For best value in General and Furnishing Ironmongery, Tools and Cutlery, all kinds of Brushes, Sporting Ammunition, Aluminium and Enamel Goods. Garden Tools. Lawn Mowers by all leading Makers.

23, NEW STREET, WELLINGTON.

Telephone 445

When the proprietor of an established business was due to retire, the opportunity arose either to change the use of the premises entirely or, more often, for a new proprietor to take advantage of any goodwill the previous incumbent had established. So it was with Mr. Cotton who continued in the same hardware line as his predecessor, Mr. Shoebotham.

Mary Brown (left) and Winnie Churm outside M.H. Brown & Son's pet shop on Mill Bank.

The capped brick pillars on the left of the photograph fronted the original Roman Catholic church and school, the former buildings of which were used as the Picture Pavilion cinema from 1911 to 1927.

The Green Man public house, run by George Davies in 1930 and H. Freeman later in the decade, was attached to the right hand side of Brown's shop.

The whole row of properties, together with a terrace of cottages which once stood between the Green Man and the entrance to Bank Road, was demolished several years ago to enable a small street of houses to be built along this stretch of Mill Bank and in a new cul de sac called Green Man Close running northwards.

F.W. Woolworth's American-origin 3*d* and 6*d* 'Fancy Bazaar' opened around 1931 in New Street. The first manager is seen here with his staff of uniformed shop assistants. The store closed in 2009.

Tom 'Rocker' Shaw's shop (above, in the 1920s) began in 1853 as a much larger furniture and fancy goods warehouse but this later specialised in jewellery and optical products. Thought to be the first shop in town to benefit from electric lighting, it became Burton's chemist's shop around 1930.

George Harvey's double-fronted jewellery shop at 4 Market Street was another of the major silversmiths in town, also selling (and repairing) watches and clocks. Note the external gas lighting still there in the 1920s.

Shops on The Green during the early 1920s. From the left: T.G. Newman's decorating and plumbing, J.A. Richards hairdressing, Arnold's saddles, harnesses, toys and sports items (formerly the Castle Inn) and W. Bailey's auctioneering premises. The Green was the centre for town markets until 1864.

The National Provincial Bank replaced all the properties shown in the top photograph when it was built in 1926. Although now called Natwest Bank, the appearance has altered little over the years.

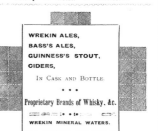

A selection of advertisements relating to drink production, delivery and sale extracted from *John Jones & Son's 1937 Directory of Wellington and District*, price: sixpence. Wellington catered well for those wishing to quench their thirst.

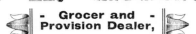
The absence of home refrigerators required fresh food to be purchased on an almost daily basis. Consequently, small grocery and confectionery shops could be found in almost any street, even on roads which were some distance from the town centre, like the Post Office on Mill Bank.

People needed clothing, often hand made rather than 'off the peg'. They also had to have their hair cut and buy health products to look their best when being photographed at, for example, a wedding or social occasion. Tradesmen satisfied those needs.

Small businesses provided a wide range of services for the benfit of their customers. Many involved traditional craftsmanship, others catered for the necessities of life. Only one enterprise survives: the High Street scrap metal firm continued by James Rollason after founder Mike Welch retired in 1930.

FRANK ARTHUR,

Family Grocer and Provision Dealer,

Market Street. - Wellington.

F. D. Hartland, Victoria Avenue

Avenue Stores, **WELLINGTON**

J. T. DRURY,

Wholesale and Retail

PURVEYOR of MEAT

First-class quality only supplied.

All orders receive personal and prompt attention.

Market Street, Wellington

TELEPHONE 93.

Telephone No. 71.

ESPLEY'S,

THE SHROPSHIRE HAM AND :-: BACON CURERS, :-: FOR

Home-Cured Hams, Bacon, Sausage and Pork Pies.

Noted throughout the Midlands.

BUY AND RELY ON OUR GOODS.

20 New Street, Wellington.

ALSO AT CEFN, OSWESTRY AND RHYL.

ESTABLISHED 1887.

THE

Wrekin Registry Office

FOR LADIES AND MAIDS.

The Registry with a Reputation.

Hours : 10-12 and 2-6. Wed. 10-1.

Note the Address—

Mrs. Espley, Wrekin Registry,

34 Wrekin Road, Wellington.

F. H. ARNOLD

SADDLER & HARNESS MAKER,

SPORTS OUTFITTER.

Church Street, Wellington, Salop.

Games and Toys, the largest selection in the district. Agent for Meccano and Hornby Trains. Bags, Trunks and Fancy Goods in all varieties, to suit all pockets. You are invited to call and look round our store.

ESTABLISHED 1850. TELEPHONE 85.

Telephone 186.

A. L. MEAKIN,

 ## Fishmonger. - Poulterer. etc.

MARKET ST., WELLINGTON.

Fresh Supplies of Fish Daily.

Poultry killed to order.

 # SWAN HOTEL,  WATLING STREET, WELLINGTON.

Phone : (Garage) 162.

Proprietor : E. REESE.

Close to Town Football Ground.

and on the Cross Roads to Shrewsbury, Bridgnorth, and North Wales.

This old-established hostelry, dating back to the 15th century, is replete with every convenience for the comfort of motorists, tourists and cyclists. Spacious Dining and other rooms.—Large or Small Parties catered for. Boarding Terms by arrangement. Noted for Butler's Ales, Stout and Spirits.

AGENT FOR MOTOR BUS TICKETS ; LONDON TO LLANDUDNO.

Another assortment of small firms trading in Wellington in the early 1930s. The Swan Hotel was blessed with the ghost of Humphrey the ostler who would eventually be exorcised in 1960, shortly before the premises were demolished. The Wrekin Registry Office acted as an employment agency.

Wellington witnessed a remarkable expansion in property development, particularly from the late 1920s onwards. Competition to attract potential buyers wishing to purchase or improve their homes led many firms (including insurance brokers) to advertise extensively in town directories, such as those produced by John Jones at The Lawns Printing Works, Park Street.

Chapter Five

Particular People

It could be said that the 1920-1939 period saw the demise of real 'people of note', whose legacies would be remembered long after they had passed on. This is not to say there have been none since, but times have changed over the past seventy years. The town is considerably larger now and modern fixations with 'busy lifestyles', television programmes, mobile communication devices and countless other distractions have contributed towards a reduction in face-to-face social interaction and participation.

Wellington had its fair share of characters whose activities were memorable for one reason or another. Some were men who made their fortunes in business; others were shop keepers who gave good service to their customers; a few gave much time and effort in trying to improve the town and the lives of its citizens; at least one came from what might be regarded as the lowest layer in a class-conscious society; and another a woman worthy of special mention. Each one played an important role in town life and their inclusion in this chapter in no way minimises the invaluable contributions made by others mentioned elsewhere.

George Evans, born 24th June 1923, seen here with the family pet in 1934 when George was a keen member of Wellington 3rd Scout Troop.

After an unhappily memorable time serving in the British army during the 'Last World War', George taught geography at Prince's Street Junior School and ended his teaching career at Orleton Park School.

He was also involved in local politics, serving as chairman of Wellington Urban District Council, and is currently president of both Wellington Civic Society and Wellington History Group.

George, a Fellow of the Royal Geographical Society, lives beneath the shadow of and is closely associated with his beloved Wrekin Hill. He celebrated his 90th birthday with a gathering of friends in the annex to the Red Lion Hotel on Holyhead Road.

Harold William Male, MA (Cantab), was very nearly the only headmaster to serve the Boys' High school in King Street for the whole of its existence from 1912 to 1940.

After gaining a degree in Classics, he taught for 14 years before moving from Bridlington School, Yorkshire to become headmaster of the newly-opened High School for Boys in Wellington. Pupil numbers increased from 36 to 84 in 1914, and plans for a new school were thwarted when war broke out. It would be another 26 years before the replacement Boys' Grammar school opened, by which time Mr. Male's school had 184 pupils in a building designed for 120.

While relations with his opposite number, Miss E.B. Ross, at the Girls' High school were strained, he was considered firm but fair, and pupils attained high levels of academic and sporting achievement under his guidance.

Always ready to help any worthy public cause, he was an Urban District Councillor for six years and helped the Cottage Hospital. Retiring through ill health in July, he died the following month on 24th August 1938.

Founder of Wellington College in 1880, John Bayley (1852-1952) was born at Ashton Under Lyne, seventh son of a seventh son; his father was a coal miner. He took up teaching at the age of 13 and, at the age of 24 came to Wellington as headmaster of Constitution Hill County school.

In 1880, he decided to found his own 'Educational Institute' at his home in Albert Road. It became known as Wellington College and, when he retired in 1920 (after which the school was renamed Wrekin College), it had grown to cover 125 acres. He lived for a while afterwards at Buckatree Hall on Ercall Lane.

A keen sportsman, he played for Wellington Town F.C. in the late 1870s and, among many charitable acts, donated premises for starting the Comrades of the Great War (Wellington) Club (currently named Sir John Bayley Club) at 23 Haygate Road in 1921.

He received his Knighthood in the New Year's Honours list of 1921. In retirement, he maintained a keen interest in educational, sporting and political matters. His grave lies in the churchyard of St. Tudno at Llandudno.

Members of the wealthy and politically influential Groom family on the steps of their Dothill Park home, August 1923. Ernest Groom, whose grandfather Richard founded the timber business which enriched the family, stands in the doorway. J.W. Clift, seated centre, married Ernest's sister Harriet.

John Wesley Clift was a forceful man, highly motivated and with a talent for getting things done but not always acting with tact or diplomacy.

Nevertheless, his managerial gifts and achievements were recognised by many members of the community at large and the Wesleyan Methodist Church in particular, where he ran the Sunday school with well meaning but uncompromising diligence.

Clift (after whom Clift Crescent is named) had his own business as a horse-drawn vehicle manufacturer on Tan Bank and is credited with inventing the (unpatented) up-and-over garage door.

He served on Wellington Urban District Council for some 41 years (retiring in 1937 on advice from his doctor), having previously been a Town Improvement Commissioner, which gave him over 50 years of service to the public.

He devoted a considerable amount of time and effort promoting improvements to the town as well as providing practical support to charitable causes. He died in 1939.

Tom Steventon (1858-1938) was a well known florist, fruiterer and seedsman, and part-time gardener for wine merchant's widow Mary Jane Slaney at Sunnycroft where, in 1901, Tom's daughter Sarah Ellizabeth worked as a housemaid. On her death in 1910, Mrs. Slaney thought enough of Tom to bequeath him £100 in her will.

Tom's business premises were at 95 New Street; his son William became a tailor at 7 Church Street. Between 1894 and 1906, while employed at Sunnycroft, he won *inter alia* prizes for his ferns, roses, pears and apples at Shropshire Horticultural Shows.

Tom, committed to serving the community and being involved with public institutions like the Poor Law Guardians Committee, held various important positions, including chairman, of the Urban District Council for 37 years from its beginning in 1894.

In recognition of his service to the town, Steventon Road was named after him.

Tom, seated, is pictured with his family in 1935.

George William Harvey (1859-1939) ran his own jeweller's and optician's business at double-fronted 4 Market Street. It had been established in 1860 by his Orkneys-born father John who moved to Wellington after learning the clock and watch making trade in Edinburgh.

George was born in 1859 and joined his father in the family firm. He qualified as an optician in 1898 and, following death of his own son, William, in the Great War, George appointed a manager to run the jewellery shop in Market Street and opened an optician's shop in 7 Crown Street. He later moved back into Market Street and appointed a manager to the optician's shop.

Mr. Harvey was a Freeman of the City of London, a member of the Shropshire County Council, Justice of the Peace, governor of the High and other schools, and served as a Wellington Urban District Councillor for over 36 years from its inception in 1894.

Harvey Crescent, originally part of the council estate on the eastern fringe of Wellington, is named after him.

Bessie Owen or, as she was known by the etiquette of the day, Mrs. John O. Owen, was a woman whom people of all ages looked up to and whose words, beliefs and thoughts influenced more than a few to lead better lives than they might otherwise have done.

She had the gift of gaining the undivided attention of audiences, and a habit of tapping a pen or pencil on the table to emphasise essential points in her talks.

Church organist for a period, she was Leader of the Men's Bible Class and Women's Society Class at New Street Wesleyan Methodist Church for over 50 years. Her husband, for many years a partner in the Steeraway Lime Company, also became involved in the classes, giving whatever support was needed.

In 1943, following her death, a marble memorial tablet was erected in the Church Room stating: 'This memorial is erected by the members of her classes in happy remembrance of their beloved leader and friend, for the inspiration of her ministries.'

Pictured outside the Station Hotel mustering support for the election which made him Conservative MP for The Wrekin in 1920, General Charles Vere Ferrers Townshend was hailed as a hero for his exploits during the Siege of Kut in 1916. Then reports surfaced revealing gross ineptitude as a soldier and the extent of the lies he had told when his soldiers were murdered in captivity while he was being treated comfortably by the Turks. He resigned as MP in 1922 and died in shame two years later.

Edith Picton-Turbervill (1872-1960) was Labour MP for The Wrekin constituency between 1929 and 1931. Serving for about the same length of time as the infamous General Townshend, Edith, by contrast, was a trustworthy woman of strong character and unwavering belief. She was a social reformer, writer and campaigner for women's rights, and was the first woman to sit on the ecclesiastical committee of parliament.

Edith worked with the poor at Shoreditch and the Vale of Glamorgan, and spent six years in India before returning to promote the YWCA of which she became president for 10 years. She is perhaps best remembered for introducing the *Sentence of Death (Expectant Mothers) Bill* which became law and enacted that no pregnant woman should be executed.

The most notable local chemist in the 1920s and '30s was that of Bates & Hunt which had two pharmacies in the town: in Market Square and New Street. Founder James Bates started as a grocer and chemist around 1850 and eventually went into partnership with Joshua Hunt.

Joshua's son Frederick E. Hunt (left, 1879-1943) ultimately controlled the firm and expanded certain aspects, like photographic processing and home brewing/wine making, as well as more specialised areas like petro-chemicals, agricultural fertilisers, to supplement traditional human and animal medicine.

Bates & Hunt had other outlets at Ironbridge, Hadley, Much Wenlock and Shifnal. The chemist shops continued to trade for decades after Fred died in a motorcycle accident; they closed around 2000.

Born in 1892, Joseph Profit Millichap started work at 14 at Penbedw Hall, Mold. After gaining experience at various other halls, he was appointed head gardener at Wellington (later Wrekin) College in 1918 where he stayed for the next 45 years.

During that period, the extent of the college expanded considerably and Joseph was responsible for laying out new grounds requiring, on at least one occasion, a new road layout to add to visual impact.

Once Vice-President of the Shropshire Horticultural Society Committee, and awarded a long service medal by the Royal Horticultural Society, in 1930 he created new playing fields on nine acres of ground.

One of founder John Bayley's dreams was to create a school within a garden. Mr. Millichap was the man who made that dream a reality.

Jack Owen was one of several men's outfitters trading in Wellington in the early 1900s. He served his apprenticeship at Venables, a large shop on the corner of Tan Bank and Walker Street.

Invariably smartly dressed, Jack's clients often admired his clothes and ordered similar ones for themselves! And he would travel in a pony and trap to obtain orders from farming customers. Eventually he was able to open his own shop (the timber framed building in Market Square), later moving round the corner into Duke Street where he employed four promising 'special assistants' to help with measuring, cutting and fitting.

In time, each of those assistants would open their own businesses whose success owed much to Mr. Owen; they were Joe Dickenson, Fred Bean, Jack Kearton and George Wem.

Taking over the prominent 'ready money' drapery business previously owned by Mr. Yeomans in Market Square in 1900, Henry Baxter soon earned a reputation for selling the good quality products at reasonable prices.

In time, he was able to employ six assistants who were expected to work hard for their pay, encouraged by his 'Spiffs Premium' incentive scheme which gave them a bonus every month. An errand boy delivered parcels and disposed of rubbish.

Henry devised his own peculiar labelling system for pricing remnants and old stock for disposal during periodic sales, and staff needed to understand the system if they were to benefit from them. Mr Baxter never bought in sub-standard items especially for his sales, a fact appreciated by loyal customers.

Born at Hack Green, Cheshire and winning a scholarship to Nantwich Grammar school, Fred Bean was apprenticed for the customary seven years to Stretch & Harlech at their large men's outfitting establishment, also at Nantwich.

Moving to Wellington c. 1906, he was trained further by Jack Owen for a few years, after which he decided the time was right to branch out for himself. His first shop was in Crown Street where he and his family lived, as many tradesmen did at that time, above the shop. He relocated to New Street, where he concentrated on selling hats and hosiery, and even ventured into the realm of gentlemen's jewellery, like cuff links and tiepins.

Fred's shop windows were renowned for their artistic displays, essential in attracting customers.

John Thomas Jervis, whose name appears several times elsewhere in these pages, was a well-known coach proprietor who began at the Old Incline in Wrockwardine Wood in the late 1920s and moved to Wellington, where business prospects were better, in the early 1930s. The motto on his business cards at the time was 'Speed with Comfort'.

His enterprise started with a single coach but towards the end of the 1950s his fleet had grown to six vehicles which were kept in a garage on ground at the intersection of Mill Lane and Regent Street.

Competition between coach operators providing bus services to townships and villages around Wellington, was fierce. The situation worsened when the more organised Midland Red Omnibus Company of Birmingham joined the fray in the late 1920s.

To bring order and unity to an otherwise chaotic situation, the Shropshire Omnibus Association (which replaced the less successful Oakengates & District Small Bus Association) was formed in the early 1930s, with John Jervis as a founder member and a director of the group for over 30 years.

Noah Frost (1868-1938) left, with daughter Elsie Price and son Ernest Frost in the yard of his bakery and grocery shop in New Street, opposite the Three Crowns pub, in 1935.

His adult children made regular rounds (using horse drawn covered waggons) delivering to all parts of the town as well as to nearby Hadley, Ketley and Admaston. A few local doctors without their own transport occasionally obtained lifts to visit patients.

Horses were taken to a nearby field (now part of the town cemetery off Linden Avenue) to graze overnight before being brought back to the bakery for the next morning's deliveries … except Sundays which Noah, a staunch Methodist, believed in 'keeping holy'.

During the 1926 General Strike, which caused much misery to a considerable number of families, Noah delivered bread to starving children in particularly hard-hit places like Ketley Brook, on the strength of promissory notes from the Miner's Union which he knew would never be honoured. He was right; wads of these notes were discovered, never to be paid, after his death in June 1938.

Tom Austin (seen here with wife Alice) was a prominent newsagent in Wellington for several decades. By the close of the 1930s, his mini-empire included four shops located in one of the stores fronting the Market Hall along Market Street, and at 45 High Street and 19 Church Street. The fourth was at 44 High Street, Hadley.

But Tom's wasn't an ordinary newsagent's. Besides the customary array of newspapers, magazines, stationery, gramophone records, tobacco products and sweets, he also ran a 'circulating library' and offered photographic services, including films, developing and enlarging in conjunction with one of the chemists in town.

As well as serving the paying public, advertising, 'Up in the morning, your Papers on Breakfast Table. Try Us!', Tom's business also acted as wholesale distributors for other newsagents in the locale.

Tom Austin's small range of picture postcards featuring scenes in and around Wellington are now collectors' items and help with historical research.

Many anecdotes surround the life of Snooks, a ginger-haired drover with 'funny' eyes who lodged in High Street and was thought to have an equally eccentric drover brother nicknamed Joker. His surname was probably Snook.

Some thought he had been abandoned by a passing circus, others that his father had been a civil engineer in the area during the 1860s. Eye witnesses claimed he had been a clown in Sanger's Circus and was an able swimmer, often to be seen diving in a nearby canal.

Whatever the truth, his name and exploits live on. Those who knew him recognised an appreciation of drink, and trustworthy reliablility as a drover.

Strangely for a man responsible for driving animals like cattle and sheep for several days along country lanes from farms to Wellington Smithfield (and back again after sales), he couldn't count in the conventional 1, 2, 3, etc., way. Instead, his unique system was thus: 'There's one, and another, and another ...'.

Yet he never lost an animal entrusted to his care. He died in 1933.

Until some time after the Second World War, it was quite normal for men to work well after reaching the age of 65. Membership subscriptions to Works pension schemes (like that introduced by Sankeys of Wellington Ltd.) began to gain popularity during the 1930s.

According to a 1939 edition of the *Wellington Journal*, which published this photograph of Jack Jordon (should it have been 'Jordan'?) demonstrating his skills as a bowl turner using the traditional old-fashioned pole, Jack was 72 years old and had worked at Richard Groom & Son's timber yard for almost 50 years, and had never lost a day's work through illness. He was one of only a handful of workers in the country who could still turn bowls using the pole lathe.

In 1938, Jack had appeared at the Royal Show at Wolverhampton but the Groom's stand at the 1939 Royal Agricultural Show at Windsor attracted the attention of King George VI and Queen Elizabeth. Canadian visitors were also fascinated by Jack's skills, and many took photographs for subsequent exhibitions and shows in Canada.

To some, working beyond what might be regarded as 'retirement age' was an accepted way to keep body and mind active, stave off boredom and make a little extra cash to pay for the little comforts of life.

Many, like Mr. H. Painter who lived with his son Richard at 59 Mill Bank, was 82 years old in 1939 and still working as a jobbing gardener for five or six days each week at several 'gentlemen's residences' in the town.

He had arrived in Wellington almost 50 years earlier, having been a farm hand at Diddlebury in south Shropshire, and worked as coachman-gardener to solicitor J.V.T. Lander at several homes until the Landers moved to Sunnycroft (now a National Trust property) on Holyhead Road where he was employed for the best part of 30 years. When progress advanced a little too speedily, Mr. Painter declined to learn how to drive 'mechanically propelled vehicles', much preferring a well-turned-out 'carriage and pair of high-stepping cobs'.

Mr. Painter also served as sidesman at All Saints parish church.

Owen Downey ('O.D.') Murphy (1874-1943), seen in his robes and regalia during the exceptional four years he served as Mayor of the Borough of Wenlock, 1928 to 1932. For much of his life O.D. was heavily involved in supporting charities and sporting clubs.

His career began as a pop salesman for R. White & Son of Smethwick and ended as head of the dominant Shropshire drinks company which incorporated the Wrekin Brewery and associated pop works in Wellington, and the important licence to deal in wines and spirits.

O.D.'s pop-making began with Long's Brewery, Ironbridge, in 1904, followed by subsequent moves to Mill Bank, Watling Street and Holyhead Road as his business interests expanded, even to the point of bottling milk produced on his farms. In the 1920s he acquired the Wrekin Brewery and the Red Lion (formerly Mill Fields) Brewery as well as other minor breweries and mineral water enterprises, until there was no competition left in this part of the county. His sons Graham and Ronald continued to run the business after his death until 1966 when the Wrekin Brewery was taken over by Greenall Whitley.

Lieutenant-Colonel James Baldwin-Webb, TD (Territorial Officers' Decoration) (1894-1940) served as Conservative Member of Parliament for The Wrekin from 1931 until his death on 18th September, 1940.

He had joined the 46th North Midland Divisional Train of the Royal Army Service Corps at the onset of World War I, serving on the Western Front from 1915. The French government made him a Chevalier of the Ordre du Merité Agricole in 1919 to add to other military awards.

Baldwin-Webb was a highly respected MP who did much to help his constituents, not least by inaugurating his Wrekin Party train excursions in the 1930s. He was appointed Deputy Lieutenant of Staffordshire in 1932.

James Baldwin-Webb died when the evacuee ship SS *City of Benares* taking him and women and children to Canada and America was torpedoed and sunk on 18 September, 1940. He had travelled on the ship specifically to raise funds for the war effort and persuade the then-neutral United States of America to enter the war.

The wedding of James William Davis ('Billie') to Gertrude ('Gert') Mary Bowles, 20th August, 1927. From left to right: Sybil Bowles (Gert's cousin), Leslie Hughes (of 53 Regent Street), Billie, Mabel Jones (of 76 Victoria Avenue) and Gert.

In the absence of cameras being generally available to the public, and the lack of camera portability at a time when most were so large they had to be fixed to tripods, wedding photographs tended to be taken in a professional photographic studio with the added benefit of countering any possibility of inclement weather.

At this time, the prime commercial photographers in Wellington were W. Cooper-Edmonds at 14 New Street, A.E. Bloomer at 8 Watling Street and relative newcomer Thomas Smith at 173 Regent Street, the latter of whom made a point of advertising 'Wedding and other Groups and Out-door work a speciality', as if to show how different he was to his competitors.

By the early 1930s, W. Cooper-Edmonds retired and photographers from *Wellington Journal* were now offering on-site wedding photography as a regular service. Consequently, they soon dominated the wedding and 'group' (i.e. society and club events) market.

The photograph of the wedding of William Leslie ('Les') Frost to Mary Jones (born Griffiths) on Sunday 4 October, 1936, was taken on the steps of New Street Methodist Church (demolished in November 2003). The photo shows relatives of the groom, with the bride's mother between Les and Mary. Charlie Parton was best man, May James the older bridesmaid and Ida Price, Les's niece, the younger.

The reception took place at J.W. Heath's Café in New Street, which catered especially for them that Sunday as Mr. Heath's business had been helped in the past during times of financial hardship by Les's baker father Noah. Sunday trading was anathema to churchgoers.

The reception for 37 people (including the cake costing £2 7s 6d) came to £7 9s 3d!

William ('Will') Picken (1898-1957) was a life-long Methodist and Trustee of New Street Wesleyan Methodist Church. He was also a lay preacher and member of the Wellington choir living at 58 Victoria Avenue, Wellington, with his wife Laura.

Will became Superintendent of the Methodist morning Sunday school. Children met in the wooden Institute buildings at the rear of the church, then went into the church for part of the morning service, leaving before the sermon to disperse into their age-separated classes until the end of the service.

The Superintendent of the afternoon Sunday school, John Wesley Clift, held that office until ill health obliged him to retire, whereupon Will was 'promoted' his replacement, and Leslie Frost took over as Superintendent of the morning school, a position he held until Will's death in 1957, at which time the running of both morning and afternoon schools merged under Leslie's leadership.

Will worked for 45 years at Allied Ironfounders, ultimately as Works Manager, and had been wounded at the Battle of the Somme in 1916.

Mr. & Mrs. J.W. Thomas, greengrocers of 75 New Street and the Market Hall celebrated their 50th wedding anniversary in 1938. Mr. Thomas had worked at Groom's timber yard and was awarded the Egyptian Medal and Star for service with 53rd Foot, K.S.L.I., which he had joined in 1881.

| **DANCING**
at The "Palais"

every

THURSDAY
& SATURDAY
to

FRED WHITELEY
AND HIS BAND

7.30 p.m. — 11.0 p.m.

ADMISSION   2/- | **PALAIS-DE-DANSE**
WELLINGTON

A Grand
Olde Tyme
Ball

Organiser: J. Lees

Music by
KATH CANNON & HER
OLDE TYME ORCHESTRA

Friday,
8th October

Modern Lounge & Buffet

DANCING
8 p.m. until midnight

M.C.: T. JACQUES |

PROGRAMME	**PARTNERS**
1. Waltz	
2. Military Two Step	
3. Veleta	
4. Eva Three Step	
5. St. Bernards Waltz	
6. Bradford Barn Dance (Spot)	
7. Royal Empress Tango	
8. Saunter	
9. Lancers	
10. Tango Waltz	
INTERVAL	
11. Marine Four Step	
12. Blues Glide	
13. Waltz Cotillion	
14. Ladbrooke	
15. Russian Ballet	
16. Blue Danube Waltz	
17. Prog. Rosy Two Step (Spot)	
18. Moonlight Saunter	
19. Anniversary Tango	
20. Quadrilles	
21. Jazz Twinkle	
22. Last Waltz	
The National Anthem	

Shrewsbury Patrons please note :—

"ENTERPRISE" HIRE SERVICE BUS will pick up as follows :—

7.30 p.m.   Harlescott
7.35 p.m.   Railway Station
7.45 p.m.   Technical College

Admission - 3/-.

Inter-war evening dances, or 'Balls' as they were still called in the late 1930s, were a perennial favourite among adults. The Palais-de-Danse in New Street attracted high numbers of folk on a regular basis (it was superseded by the Majestic Ballroom). Dance cards like this from 1937 ensured ladies weren't double-booked for particular numbers, or (by drawing a line through specific dances) they could avoid unfamiliar routines. Note the inclusion of the National Anthem at the end of the evening.

The Wrekin Syncopated Orchestra was one of several semi-professional musical groups to perform at private functions as well as in public theatres in the 1920s.

Chapter Six

Social Scene

The majority of people in Wellington did their best to resume normal life as soon as possible after the end of Great War hostilities. Those who survived the horrors of the badly managed conflict, or witnessed the suffering and deprivation locally, were undoubtedly affected by their experiences. Nevertheless, human nature is such that ways were found of coping and forgetting and looking to the future. Even the post-war worldwide influenza epidemic could only delay hopes for a better future.

The town was fortunate to have so many talented and willing volunteers to organise well-supported activities ranging from theatrical performances (both professional and amateur) to large scale outdoor attractions. These community-spirited people, together with impressive developments in the realm of purpose-built leisure facilities, considerably widened the scope for public entertainment during the interwar years.

Whereas children were perfectly capable of finding their own amusement with the minimum of toys, teenagers and adults relished the challenge of taking part in all manner of cultural pursuits, and often went to great lengths to create their own costumes or did their best to achieve near-perfect performances. Adding to the cultural mix were live performances of a theatrical or musical nature staged by professionals who came to perform in the town.

Because of the increasing variety of entertainment throughout this period, Wellington became a magnet for folk from neighbouring towns and villages. Not only was the town's position as the most important centre for commerce, banking and shopping unchallenged at this time but all the major sources of leisure entertainment were located here. Other local townships had their own cinemas, for example, but the size and capabilities of those in Wellington were unsurpassed.

By the start of the 1920s, it was as if people were fed up with almost thirty years' worth of economic uncertainty, one war after another and an oppressive cloud created by international tensions. Wellingtonians, like folk in other British towns, wanted a period of social improvement ... and did their best to attain this goal.

The 1920s witnessed further economic and social upheaval in the form of the General Strike of 1926 as well as rises and falls in unemployment corresponding with similar peaks and troughs in other western countries. The early years of the 1930s saw the situation improve, a fact supported by the fact that community entertainments became more ambitious, and substantial sums were invested in developing the cinematic and theatrical scene.

Children eating apples while playing together at The Paddock, Wrockwardine Road in 1935. From left to right: Don Houlston, Joan Bevan, Florence Bevan, Marion Bevan, Roma Bevan, Jack Bevan, Brian Houlston (apparently sitting on a Great Western Railway boundary post) and Ken Scott.

Primary teachers at New Street Wesleyan Methodist Sunday school with Superintendent John Wesley Clift on the annual 'treat' via horse-drawn waggons to Crudgington, Saturday, 13th July, 1929. From left to right: Nellie Cole, Mary Jones (in front), Hilda Moore, ? Tinsley, Florrie Jones, Maggie Childs.

Patrol Leaders of Wellington Methodist Girl Guides at The Manse, 181 Holyhead Road, c. 1929.
Back row, from left to right: Mary Postans, Evelyn Barefoot, Mary Jones. Front: Eunice Barnes,
Monica Woodward, Joan Heywood.

'British Empire' Concert Party, Methodist Institute, February 1939. From left to right: Ian Fenn,
Desmond Evans, Margaret Fenn, Joan Picken, Gwen Picken, Joan Price, Kathleen Hesketh,
Mary Morris, Marjorie Cotton, Nancy Sumnall, Gwen Jones (kneeling, left), Doreen Sumnall,
Dorothy Fenn (Britannia), Evelyn Sumnall, Ida Price, Cynthia Whiteway (kneeling, right), Rose
Titley behind Peggy Price, Margaret Morris, Ethel Holding, Evelyn Jervis, Pat Morgan, Douglas
Morgan.

Wellington Guides and Scouts at All Saints parish church, possibly after a commemorative service in the late 1920s. One scout is thought to be D. or S. Briers. Among the guides are Ruth Warne, Marjorie Darrall, Marjorie McCrea, Nellie Allman (behind right flag), Mrs. Lander (Divisional Guide), Mrs. Mary Leake, Louise Pearce, Peggy Laddiman and Mrs. Ward (from Hiatt's Ladies' College).

Rangers Section, 2nd Wellington Girl Guides, 1930s. Back row, from left to right: Nellie Allman, Nora Vickers, Beattie Shelton, Gladys Crow, Doris Shelton, Marjorie Darrall, Evelyn Morgan. Front: Rachel Stokes, Mary Leake, Capt. Ruth Warne, Lieut. Norah Shoebotham, Monica Powell, May Wall.

Wellington Cubs and Scouts, late 1930s. Adults on the front row are, from the left, Nora Vickers, Scoutmaster Lewis, Revd John Hayes, Alan Borders and Mrs. Lewis. The boys include three Morgans, two Wards, two McCormicks, Harrison, Jackson, Stokes, Williams, Dennis Ball, Eddie Bentley, Bill Dabbs, Desmond Evans, Ian Fenn, Don Houlston, Clive Tipton, Fred Taylor, Raymond Teece.

A society ladies' tea party was held in the grounds of Lieut.-Col. James Patchett's Haybridge Hall on 26 June, 1921. The event was hosted by his daughters with their maids. Among those attending were Mrs. Capes, Deakin, Delves, Holland, Millard, Price and two Mrs. Willets (senior and junior).

Cast of the Pierrot Concert staged by the Union Free church, Constitution Hill, in March 1934. Among the performers are Maggie and Winnie Judson and Wellington decorator William Newman. Four years later, the church choir gave a performance of *Cinderella*.

Youngsters from New Street Wesleyan Methodist church take part in a concert party produced by Elsie Price in the 1930s. Elsie's husband Jack, a carpenter at C. & W. Walker's Midland Iron Foundry at Donnington, made the rifles; they would be used in other productions, including pantomimes.

Competion between GWS (Great Western Railways) and LMS (London Midland Scottish) railway companies and the Midland Red omnibus company for the provision of holiday excursions was keen. Consequently, there was plenty of opportunity for travellers to benefit from cheap prices.

Local bus operators also provided their own 'motor coach tours', often with open-topped charabancs. Here, Marjorie McCrea (centre, back) sits between Norah Shoebotham (left) and her mother Louisa Florence McCrea, on a trip to Weston-super-Mare in the 1930s.

Throughout the 1930s, Annual Wrekin Parties were organised by Member of Parliament for The Wrekin, Lieutenant-Colonel James Baldwin-Webb.

Each year, thousands of people boarded chartered trains. Booklets provided all the detail they needed to know about their special day excursion. Coloured badges, bearing the name and colour of the train allocated to each person together with the face of Baldwin-Webb himself, helped promote the smooth running of the event.

Over the years, folk visited Southampton and the Isle of Wight, the Aldershott Tattoo (twice), the Royal Tournament, the Houses of Parliament and, in 1935, the King's Silver Jubilee celebrations in the Albert Hall, London.

'The Wrekin Outing' report in a May 1938 edition of *Wellington Journal* included a number of photographs such as this showing the wonderful time folk had on a day trip to Scotland. Over 5,000 constituents and other Shropshire residents visited the Empire Exhibition at Glasgow. Lieut-Col. Baldwin-Webb believed in giving value for money, so everyone also took a cruise on the River Clyde to see the area's outstanding beauty for themselves. No trip had taken place in 1937, and the 1938 excursion proved to be the last.

WELLINGTON & DISTRICT Y.M.C.A.

Carnival Parade.

JULY 26th, 1924.

PRESIDENT :—LIEUT.-COL. H. L. OLDHAM, D.S.O.
CHAIRMAN :—MR. J. E. BULLOCK.
TREASURER :—MR. J. SYDNEY SMITH.
SECRETARY :—MR. J. T. TURNER.

—:o:—

*Competitors assemble on Roslyn Road, at 1-45.
Judging will take place at 2 o'clock.*

—:o:—

*THE PROCESSION will move at **2-30** and proceed
to King Street, Regent Street, Mill Fields, Watling
Street, Mill Bank, High Street, Victoria Street, King
Street, Park Street, Church Street, Queen Street, Bridge
Road, Walker Street, Crown Street, Market Square,
Church Street, Vineyard Road and to the Field on
Spring Hill.—Halts will be made for Dancing Displays,
&c., in Millfields, bottom of New Church Road, The
Green and The Market Square.*

—:o:—

*Officials may be recognised by Coloured Rosettes :
Chairman—Red. Treasurer—Mauve. Secretaries—Pale Blue.
Marshal—Orange. General Secretary—Royal Blue.*

—:o:—

**The following Ladies & Gentlemen have kindly consented
to act as Judges :—Mrs. Blockley, Mrs. Brittain, Mrs. T.
Shaw, W. M. Gordon, Esq., Walter Dugdale, Esq., T. Thom-
son, Esq., and Dr. Wedd.**

*The Public are kindly requested to give generously
to the Collectors.*

Programmes — 1d. each.

It appears that the first Wellington Carnival took place on 26 July 1924, with the express intention of raising the morale of townsfolk as well as people living in neighbouring towns and villages (and coincidentally to raise funds for the town branch of the Y.M.C.A.), by consigning the terrible effects of the Great War to history. As shown above, the route followed by the procession was circuitous in the extreme. The event, which met with universal approval, was an enormous success. That being so, it's a mystery why the carnival concept seems to have been shelved until Wellington Town F.C. Supporters' Club began its own series of grand scale annual carnivals in June 1935.

Anyone who wanted or could be cajoled to take part in the carnival was expected to provide their own costumes and make-up.

There were no nearby costume hire shops, so eager participants had little choice but to design and make their own using whatever materials were to hand.

Three of the more impressive costumes were made by the Keay sisters (from left to right) Clara *(Aladdin and his Wonderful Lamp)*, Ida *(Jazz Pierrette)* and Violet *(Chinese Lantern)*, who lived in St. John Street.

Contestants in the Original Characters category line up for the official photograph for the 1924 Carnival. Not everyone was available (some younger participants may have been at school or performing chores in the family business).

Order of Procession.

MARSHAL :

Mr. H. D. Westley.

Court Boy	H. G. Stone, Stud Farm, Wellington.

The Lilleshall Collieries Prize Band.

Tableau	" The Raiders " (Viking Period). Lotus (Stafford) Youths' Gym. Class.

First Hadley Troupe Boy Scouts.

ORIGINAL CHARACTERS (Lady) :

ALADDIN & HIS WONDERFUL LAMP	Miss C. Keay, St. John Street.
BOY BLUE	,, Florrie Wilson, Ketley.Sands
CHINESE LANTERN ..	,, V. Keay, St. John Street.
THE FRENCH DOLL ..	,, F. Williscroft, Horsefair, Rugeley.
GIPSY FORTUNE TELLER	,, D. Padmore, Millfields.
GNOMES	Misses F. and D. Wilson, Ketley Sands.
JAZZ PIERRETTE	Miss I. Keay, St. John Street.
NO MORE STRIKES ..	,, Elsie Davies, Granville St., St. Georges.
POMPOMETTE	,, P. Phillips, Union St. Hadley
SHUTTLE COCK.. ..	,, M. Manning, Mill Bank.
THE SPIRIT OF XMAS ..	,, M. Lloyd, King St. Broseley.
TOPSEY (UNCLE TOM'S CABIN)	,, H. Williscroft, Rugeley.
EARLY VICTORIAN ..	,, L. Wilson, Ketley Sands.
YES ! WE HAVE NO BANANAS	,, J. K. Greenfield, Walker St.
CONFETTI	,, G. M. Howells, Walker St.
RED ROSE	,, K. Roberts, High Street.
ORANGES AND LEMONS ..	,, B. Davies, High Street.
EGYPTIAN FORTUNE TELLER	,, Irene Hall, Victoria Avenue.
PILLAR BOX	,, Doris Grainger, High Street.
Decorated Motor Cycle	Mr. W. E. G. Rhodes, Dawley.
Decorated Motor Car "CARNIVAL"	,, S. R. Latham and Party.
Tableau " PREVENTS THAT SINKING FEELING."	Mr. J. W. Knapton, Victoria Avenue.
Tradesmen's Turnouts ..	United Yeast Co., Ltd., Wrekin Road.
DAIRYMAN	Mr. J. S. Stone, Stud Farm.
MOTOR VAN	Messrs. G. H. Espley, New Street.
MOTOR VAN	Messrs. Morgan, Market Square.
TRADES EXHIBITION	Miss E. M. Shelton, King Street.
WIRELESS	Messrs. E. W. Jones, Market St.
MOTOR VAN	Messrs. McClure Bros., Duke St.

Female participants appearing in the collective photo-shoot on the previous page were thrilled to find their names (and those of the characters they protrayed) included in the official programme (male participants are detailed on the next page). H.D. Westley, stalwart of the town's Orchestral and Operatic Society, ensured the event passed off without a hitch.

10th Stafford (Y.M.C.A.) Troupe Boy Scouts.

The Lotus Concert Party	Lotus, Ltd., Stafford.
Siemens Morris Dancers	Stafford.
Decorated Car ..	Mr. S. C. Parker, New Church Rd.

HUMOROUS CHARACTERS (Gents) :

AUNT SALLY (Human) ..	Mr. E. W. Riddle, Plough Road.
OLD WOMAN	„ A. Payne, Park Street.
SCARECROW	„ H. Marston, Ketley.
"MISS VANITY" ..	„ E. Holford, Ketley.
{ "THE CHIMNEY SWEEP"	„ A. Smith, High Street. }
{ AND "THE MAID"	„ D. Knapton, Victoria Avn. }
GOLLIWOG	„ J. C. Morgan, Horsehay.
OLD WOMAN	„ E. Judson, King Street.
Cycles .. "Fields' Ink Imp"	Mr. W. Lowe, Oakengates.
"London Bridge"	Miss V. G. Fullerton, Shifnal.
Decorated Car "The Gondoliers"	Lotus Printing Dept., Stafford.
Y.M.C.A. Wagon.	
Tableau "SAUCY BOY" (Prevents that Gnawing Feeling)	Miss C. Knapton & Master M. Knapton.
Motor Combination "ROSES"	Mr. J. T. Price, New Street.

ORIGINAL CHARACTERS (Gents):

INDIAN BOYS ..	From Dawley.
CHINESE BOY ..	Mr. T. Jones, St. Georges.
COWBOY	„ G. Tudor, Victoria Avenue.
HARLEQUIN	„ J. Frost, King Street.
INDIAN BOY	„ W. Davies, Stafford.
JAZZ PIERRETTE ..	„ K. A. Chambers, King St.
KAFFIR BOY	„ T. R. Harris, Leegomery.
RAPIER ..	„ J. W. Hudson, Stafford.
SAMBO ..	„ G. B. Bruce, Stafford.
SIMPLE SIMON ..	„ Onions, St. Georges.
DOLL ..	„ J. Knapton, Wellington.
UNRULY BOYS ..	„ S. Davies, High Street.
Tableau "WOLF CUBS,"	Stafford Y.M.C.A. Wolf Cub Pack.

Patrol of Walsall Rover Scouts.

Jester Boys	From Dawley.
Tableau .. PROFESSORS JAZZ BAND ..	Mr. S. Barnsley, Ketley.
Collectors ..	The Lotus & Delta Collecting Teams, Stafford.
Collecting Flag	Mr. A. S. M. Northwood, Stafford.
Red, White & Blue	Miss C. Palin, Mill Bank.
Nurse	Nurse Colclough, Stafford.

Third of the four-page 1924 Carnival programme. Page four invited members of the public to enjoy entertainment at the Spring Hill Field (now the southernmost part of North Road which then belonged to the Charltons of Apley Castle's Vineyard House estate) after the parade.

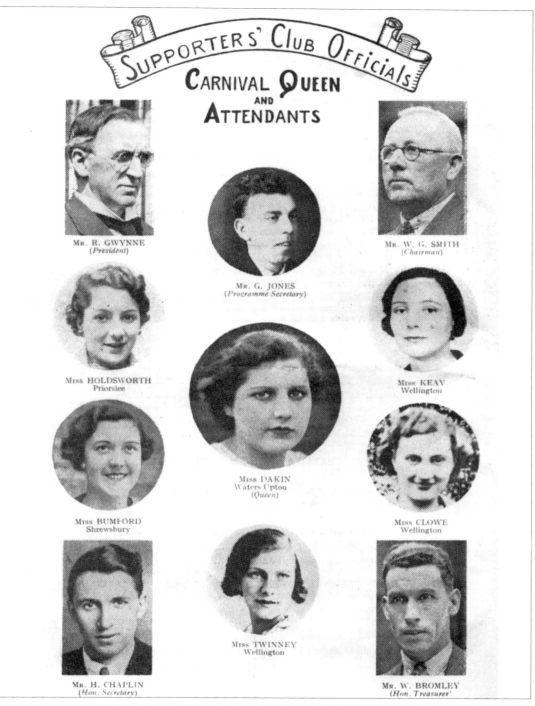

SUPPORTERS' Club Officials

CARNIVAL QUEEN AND ATTENDANTS

MR. R. GWYNNE
(*President*)

MR. G. JONES
(*Programme Secretary*)

MR. W. G. SMITH
(*Chairman*)

MISS HOLDSWORTH
Priorslee

MISS KEAY
Wellington

MISS BUMFORD
Shrewsbury

MISS DAKIN
Waters Upton
(*Queen*)

MISS CLOWE
Wellington

MR. H. CHAPLIN
(*Hon. Secretary*)

MISS TWINNEY
Wellington

MR. W. BROMLEY
(*Hon. Treasurer*)

Main personnel appearing in the Supporters' Club's third Carnival programme, 20 June, 1936. Instigated solely to 'further the cause of the Wellington Town Football Club', the event began and ended at the Buck's Head ground, with the obligatory procession around the main streets.

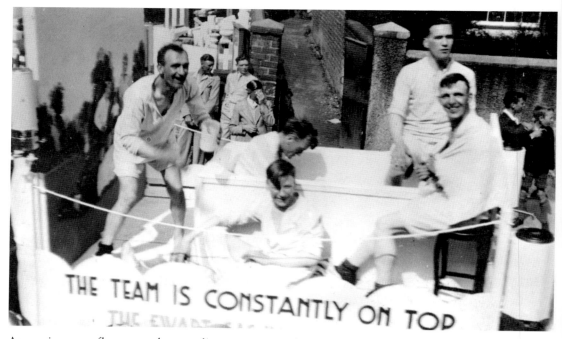

THE TEAM IS CONSTANTLY ON TOP

Appearing on a float was almost a licence to create havoc. While members of the public threw coins at the participants as their contribution towards the Carnival's fund-raising aims, those same participants revelled in hurling good-natured abuse to encourage further financial projectiles.

Horse drawn carts were loaned by local businesses to act as floats for groups presenting a diorama or scenic display. This float, guided by Arnold Harrison and 'Stick' Jones was provided by coal merchants Stockley and Tudor; the scene appears to be of a Gretna Green wedding.

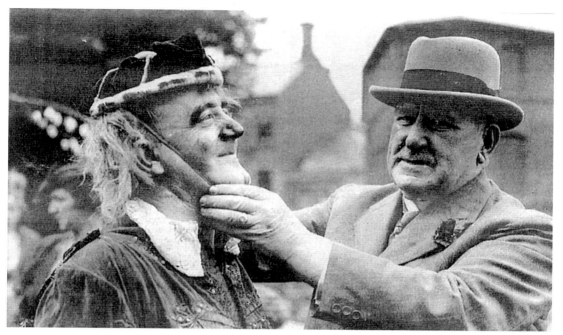

The King of Mirth was an important appointment, probably more so than that of Carnival Queen. It was in his power to grant titles (such as the Knighthood of Ketley Brook) to worthy citizens. Here, O.D. Murphy crowns Cecil Bishop at the 1938 Carnival.

The winning float from the 1937 Carnival: 'Rule Britannia' presented by residents of Horton village.

NEW LOUNGE,
BAR, SMOKE-ROOMS, DINING ROOM, LARGE CAR PARK,
PARTIES CATERED FOR.
— **TRUMAN'S FAMOUS ALES AND STOUT.** —
BREWERS SINCE 1666.

One problem in attracting new custom into pubs was enticing patrons through the main door. Sid Davies, landlord of the Park Hotel on Whitchurch Road in 1938, thought including a photograph of the relaxing interior in this *Wellington Journal* advertisement would do the job.

The Hare and Hounds at 61 Watling Street, *c.* 1920, with publican Frank Hordley in the doorway. Isaac Harris had taken over by 1922 and William Podmore by 1929. Although popular with matchgoers as it was the nearest public house to the entrance of the Buck's Head football ground, it had become a Fried Fish Saloon run by J. Reynolds sometime between 1930 and 1937.

The Cock Hotel crossroads, possibly in the late 1920s, with an RAC patrolman directing traffic. On the right is the medieval Swan Inn, rebuilt in 1960, and The Anchor Inn immediately to its left in Mill Bank; it closed in 1916. A roundabout, removed in 1958, was built here in 1937.

Charlton Arms Hotel, 1920s, opened shortly after railway passenger services served the town from 1849. It became a jewel in Wellington's crown until acquired by Nextdom, a company which allowed the hotel to close and deteriorate following a small fire in 2006. Despite its status as a Grade II Listed Building, survival is in doubt. Madame B.M. Wood's millinery shop on the right closed in the 1930s.

Picnics were and still are enjoyed on The Wrekin Hill. Here, several generations of the Pierce family relax in the mid 1920s. Elizabeth Pierce (fourth from the right) took over the Ercall Hotel and Assembly Rooms in Market Street after the death of her husband shortly before the Great War began.

View of The Wrekin Hill over Herbert Avenue from the Bowring Recreation Park, 1930s. The Park, bequeathed to the people of Wellington in 1912 by a former fishmonger in the town, became a popular venue for its playing fields, bowling green, tennis courts and children's paddling pool.

The Forest Glen Pavilion, opened and owned by the Pointon family for 100 years from 1889, benefitted from greater numbers of refreshments-seeking visitors to The Wrekin Hill once omnibuses made regular trips from outlying towns on Bank and other holidays from the 1920s onwards.

The first lorry to be driven to the summit of The Wrekin Hill was a loaded Chevrolet truck driven by Mr. Hotchkiss on 23 June 1929. It was a stunt by Vincent Greenhous, to advertise their fourth annual motor show in Shrewsbury, witnessed by thousands of spectators. It wasn't the first motor vehicle to be driven to the top: that distinction belongs to ex-RAF pilot Captain Riley, accompanied by Miss Pat Riley of 'Westcote', Wellington, in 1920 with his 11 h.p. Riley of Coventry car.

Commissionaire Harry Griffiths at the entrance to St. Patrick's church hall on Mill Bank, which became the first picture house in Wellington when it opened its silent cinematic doors to an enthralled public in 1911. It was called the Picture Pavilion.

The building was the original Catholic church in town, becoming the church hall in 1906 when the present replacement church was built at the junction of Plough Road and King Street.

Filmgoers enjoyed seeing moving pictures accompanied by impromptu music played by one of several local pianists; the projectionist was Fred Chaplin who kept a newsagent's shop, also on Mill Bank. Monkey nuts were accepted as obligatory nibbles and, although noisy behaviour was to be expected, spitting (as confirmed on the foyer notice) was prohibited.

For a while, live entertainment was provided by travelling companies supported by the cinema's own amateur Pavilion Orchestra. Charlie Chaplin's *The Gold Rush* was one of the last films shown before the Pavilion closed in 1927.

Changing film details at the Town Hall Cinema in Market Street, 1930s.

American Kay Francis (1905-1968, real name Katharine Edwina Gibbs) was a stage actress who became a film star. By the mid 1930s, she was one of the highest paid film stars in Hollywood. *Sweet Aloes,* the film title being mounted here in the illuminated display, was released in Britain in 1936, having been based on Jay Mallory's play of that name but which, when released in America, was given the name *Give Me Your Heart.* It wasn't a great success. Despite her many triumphs, because of a slight speech impediment she earned the nickname 'Wavishing Kay Fwancis'.

The Town Hall began showing (silent) films in July 1920, when musica; accompaniment was provided by pianist Miss Richards and violinists Mr. Pownall and Elsie Stinton. A sound system was installed in 1932, which completed the transition from silent movies. The Hall ceased as a cinema in 1960 by which time it had earned itself the unkind 'flea pit' soubriquet. It has since had a variety of uses.

Chapter Seven

Cinemas and Theatres

People love live theatrical performances, and Wellington has a long history of providing suitable venues from market places to purpose-built halls.

Of the theatres and cinemas in Wellington, only one has very little information to hand down the generations: The Alhambra, newly built on Tan Bank in 1927. It changed its name to The Playhouse but was short lived, probably because of competition from other establishments like the Grand Theatre. Nevertheless, it staged variety performances until its demise, since when it has been known as Rechabites Hall and, from 1937, the Billards Hall.

The Picture Pavilion, Grand Theatre (which had a variety of earlier names), the Town Hall and Clifton Cinema were the most memorable establishments.

The Town Hall was used extensively as a venue for all manner of public and private events from its creation in 1868. As well as a cinema, it also staged popular performances by national performers, like George Hector Atkinson (stage name 'Tommy') who, as well as being Musical Director of the British Ballet Organisation, was also regarded as 'another Paderewski' for his pianistic accomplishments.

The Grand Theatre, the 'Cosiest Cinema in Town' in Tan Bank. Originating in a galvanised shed previously used as an American Roller Skating Rink, it was extensively reconstructed in 1936.

Telegrams :
Grand, Wellington.
Telephone : 297.

Proprietor :
W. I. WRIGHT.

GRAND THEATRE

WELLINGTON, SHROPSHIRE.
First in 1910, foremost ever since.

A 1930s letterhead surmounts a photograph of innumerable children who were given the opportunity to celebrate King George V's Jubilee in 1935 with a free visit to the cinema (at which time a natural slope predated the steps installed in 1936) where they enjoyed a programme of films.

First impressions count ... Usherettes Pat Ford (left) and Mary Taylor greeted patrons to the Grand Theatre.

Seen here in 1938, their duties involved checking the validity of tickets, showing (via torchlight) people to their seats (the exact area depending on the price paid), maintaining order during performances, selling ice creams and soft drinks off trays suspended from straps around their necks (again by torchlight) during the Intermission, and trying to ensure (as far as possible) that folk remained standing at their seats during the playing of the National Anthem which always ended each day's performance. And tidying the auditorium to make it ready for the next performance. All this, and smiles too!

Besides running his own omnibus services, coach proprietor John Thomas Oliver Jervis, eventually of 49 Regent Street, wasn't just a businessman who enjoyed angling and nurtured a keen interest in boxing and shooting.

He was also a talented 'squeezebox' accordion player who, occasionally with his daughter Daisy (best remembered by many townsfolk and bus passengers for serving teas and home made ice cream from the Jervis café in High Street) performed semi-professionally at public entertainments. This photograph was taken in 1937.

The Society was blessed with highly motivated personnel, as well as numerous sponsors and officials. Stage manager W.J. Martin (left, sometimes replaced by J. Bullock), President Dr. George Mackie (centre) and Honorary Musical Director and Producer H.D. Westley were key players in ensuring continued support from able behind-the-scenes people, gifted musicians, actors, singers, dancers and supporting cast members and, of course, the public. The onslaught of the Second World War brought an end to what was arguably the most significant cultural event in Wellington's history.

HASSI   RED SHADOW   SID EL KAR
" Stop! I want your promise, the Sign of the Head and Heart "

Promotional scene from the programme for *The Desert Song*, featuring Hassi, the mysterious Red Shadow and Sid el Kar. The cast and musicians may have been amateurs but their performances were professional. It was the least they could do to satisfy the paying (and appreciative) audience.

Wellington Orchestral and Operatic Society.
"THE DESERT SONG."
Dramatis Personæ

SID-EL-KAR (The Red Shadow's Lieutenant)	HAROLD GREEN.
HADJI (A Riff Farmer)	FRANK EVANS.
NERI (His Wife)	PEGGY LADIMAN.
BENJAMIN KIDD (Society Correspondent for the Paris " Daily Mail ")	HARRY GEEVES
CAPT. PAUL FONTAINE (Of the French Legion) ...	PERCY MORGAN
MARGOT BONVALET (Guest of General Birabeau) ..	VAUDREY DARBY.
GENERAL BIRABEAU (Governor of a French Moroccan Province	RAYMOND CARVER.
PIERRE BIRABEAU (His Only Son)	ABE LEWIS
SUSAN (General Birabeau's Ward)	FIFI COOPER-ELMONDS
EDITH (Her Friend)	DORIS JONES.
AZURI (Ben Ali's Favourite)	DOROTHY BISIKER.
ALI BEN ALI (Caid of a Riff Tribe)	CHARLES GRIFFITHS.
CLEMENTINA (A Spanish " Lady ")	IVY MORGAN.
MINDAR ⎱ (Leading Members of the Red	⎰ ARTHUR MARTIN.
HASSI ⎰ Shadow's Band)	⎱ TOM EVANS.
LIEUT. LA VERNE (Of the French Foreign Legion)	BERT RICHARDS.
SERGEANT DE BOUSSAC (Of the French Foreign Legion)	ROWLAND HUMPHRIES.

LADIES' CHORUS of French Girls, Soldiers' Wives:

MESDAMES : L. Boughy, Evans, M. Johnstone, V. Jones, E. Lewis, G. Lewis, W. Morris, W. Potts, S. E. Westley.

MISSES : A. Bostock, J. Corbett, V. Davies, D. Harper, J. Reading, H. Roberts, S. Teece, J. E. Walker, M. Wellings.

DANCING GIRLS :

Joan Beard, L. Cossentine, Peggy Dickenson, Christin Gittins, Crystal Jones, Joyce Lloyd, Peggy Mason, Gladys Shelton, Mary Torkett, Joan Watkins.

AZURI GIRLS :

Joan Beard, Joce Corbett, Crystal Jones, Gladys Shelton.

SOLDIERS of the French Legion and Member of the Red Shadow's Band :

F. Bisiker, B. Bisiker, H. Butler, F. S. Escourt, J. R. Frost, C. Fulkes, R. Fulkes. R. C. Harding, E. L. James, E. H. Jones, E. Laddiman, J. Laddiman, J. Langford, T. Potter, G. Smith, P. Sparrow. C. S. Stevens, W. Sadler, E. Taylor, E. B. Rowlands.

Azuri Dances arranged by MISS WILLIAMS, MISS HAMMOND'S SCHOOL OF DANCING, CHESTER.

ACT I.—Scene 1	RETREAT OF THE RED SHADOW IN THE RIFF MOUNTAINS (Evening).
	Scene 2.	OUTSIDE GENERAL BIRABEAU'S HOUSE (The Same Evening).
	Scene 3	A ROOM IN GENERAL BIRABEAU'S HOUSE (A Few Minutes Later).
ACT II.—Scene 1.	THE HAREM OF ALI BEN ALI (Afternoon of the Following Day)
	Scene 2.	A CORRIDOR (A Few Minutes Later).
	Scene 3	THE ROOM OF THE SILKEN COUCH (A Few Minutes Later).
	Scene 4.	EDGE OF THE DESERT (The Following Morning, Half An Hour Before Dawn)
	Scene 5.	COURTYARD OF GENERAL BIRABEAU'S HOUSE (Two Days Later).
		Locale : NORTHERN AFRICA.

WARDROBE MISTRESSES	MESDAMES B. REEDE, S. E. WESTLEY, MISSES E. RIGBY, E. RILEY.
PROPERTY MASTER	MR. ROWLAND HUMPHRIES.
DRESSERS	MESDAMES R. HUMPHRIES, A. LEWIS.
PERRUQUIERS	MESSRS. S. C. ARLETTE, E. BARLOW, R. BARLOW, F. BISIKER, B. RICHARDS.
	MESDAMES S. E. WESTLEY, S. C. PARKER, W. J. MARTIN MISSES I. RILEY, M. JONES.
CALL BOYS	MESSRS. B. BISIKER, L. STOKES.
COSTUMES BY	B J. SIMMONS & CO., LTD., LONDON
SCENERY BY	A. WYATT & SON, WOLVERHAMPTON

THE PLAY PRODUCED AND CONDUCTED BY H D. WESTLEY.

Dramatis Personae from the penultimate Wellington Orchestral and Operatic Society production to be held at the Grand Theatre. Productions at the Grand Theatre were *The Mikado* (1927), *Yeoman of the Guard* (1928), *The Gondoliers* (1929), *Iolanthe* (1930), *Merrie England* (1932, and presented again at Orleton Park in 1936 while the Grand was being reconstructed), *Ruddigore* (1933), *Tom Jones* (1934), *The Quaker Girl* (1935), *The Desert Song* (1937) and *Maid of the Mountains* (1938). The Society's final production *"Good-night Vienna!"* (1939) was held at the Clifton.

THE

CONCERT

OF THE YEAR!

— IN THE —

CLIFTON CINEMA,
Wellington,

(BY THE COURTESY OF MR. B. S. WILLMOTT)

SUNDAY, 12th DECEMBER, 1937

TO COMMENCE AT 8 P.M.

SANKEY'S CASTLE WORKS BAND

CONDUCTOR: MR. C. YORATH.

SPECIAL ENGAGEMENT OF

Mr. HARRY MORTIMER

FAMOUS CORNET SOLOIST.

(FODEN'S BAND, HALLE ORCHESTRA & B.B.C.)

MR. H. MOORE	-	-	Bass.
MISS L. M. WRIGHT	-	Soprano.
MR. W. LAWRENCE	-	Accompanist.

The Clifton Cinema opened in 1937 in direct competition with the Grand Theatre and, to a lesser extent, the Town Hall. From the outset, it staged a wide range of cinematic, theatrical, orchestral and variety performances. Shopping Queen and other public participation events also attracted attention.

To attract attention in 1938, the Clifton ran a publicity stunt whereby 'the world's master mind reader' The Great Nixon, who was perfoming throughout the week, wore his famous blindfold to discover the hiding place of an all-wave radion set supplied by Messrs. E.W. Jones of New Street. Nixon, seen here in Market Street, located the radio inside Boyle's New Street florist's after 45 minutes.

MONDAY, JANUARY 9th   FOR 6 DAYS.

On the Stage— **SPECIAL ATTRACTION!**

SANDY LAURI presents his Grand Pantomime

"BABES IN THE WOOD"

With a Big Pantomime Cast, including

Della Neil, as Robin Hood (Our Hero),

And That Clever Mirth Purveyor, **Ran Churchill** as 'Orace (One of the Robbers).

Speciality Acts by The Derry-Fenn Babes. Les Artistiques. Will Amber. Peggy REES. Harry Gordon. The Debonaire .dies.

Continuous from 6-30 p.m.

Matinees—Monday Thursday and Saturday, at 2-30 p.m.

NO ADVANCE IN PRICES OF ADMISSION

Front Circle, 1/6.; Front Stalls and Back Circle, 1/3.; Centre and Side Stalls 1/-; Back Stalls, 6d.; Children 4d., 6d., and 1/-. (including tax).

BRING THE CHILDREN to SEE A REAL LIVE PANTOMIME.

LOVELY DELLA NEIL as Robin Hood (Our Hero).

The Clifton soon gained an enviable reputation as worthy successor to the Grand Theatre for its highly popular 'Special Attraction' live performances. Some were essentially amateur productions, others professional or semi-professional in nature. The *Wellington Journal & Shrewsbury News* became the main source of 'what's on' information, not just in the Wellington area but also throughout and beyond Shropshire. This January 1939 advertisement provides comprehensive information for prospective patrons, with the additional tag that they should 'Bring The Children'.

WILL AMBER

That "Daft" Comedian

Mimic, Singer, Whistler, Gags, Drummer, Ventriloquist, Eats Fire, etc.
——(This "Idiot" is Entirely Born to Entertain You)——

Many of the performers appearing at the Clifton were accomplished in a number of fields. The troop accompanying Will Amber, That 'Daft' Comedian Wmentioned in the *Babes in the Wood* advertisement may not be regarded as politically correct by today's standards but was highly popular at the time.

Fred Brown and page boy George with the loudspeaker van provided by Tommy Dawes of Oakengates. It was driven around town to advertise Clifton programmes. Latest hit records, changed every Monday morning, were loaned by Field's Music Depot in Station Road and played between announcements.

Line up of principal characters in the 1939 production of "*Good-Night Vienna!*". From left to right: Ernst, Vicki, Johann, Freda, Max, Greta, Mitzi, Prince Schemettoff, Wilhelmina.

"GOOD-NIGHT VIENNA!"

❧❧❧

DRAMATIS PERSONÆ

(In order of appearance).

FRIEDA ⎱	Assistants in the Flower Shop	⎰ VERA MARTIN.
VICKI ⎰		⎱ IVY MORGAN.
CAPTAIN MUNTZ		VICTOR EVANS.
HERR KLOTZ		ROWLAND HUMPHRIES.
CILLI (Errand Girl in the Flower Shop)		DOROTHY BISIKER.
ERNST ⎱	(Officers in the Imperial Guard)	⎰ BERT RICHARDS.
JOHANN ⎰		⎱ ABE LEWIS.
MAX (Son of Prince Schemettoff		WILLIAM BUCKETT.
GRETA (Manageress of the Flower Shop)		SHEILA BRANDON.
BAUMER (A Bootmaker)		HARRY HAWKINS.
HANS (A Private in the Imperial Guard)		ARTHUR MARTIN.
PRINCE SCHEMETTOFF		RICHARD HARDING.
HELGA		KATHLEEN COXON.
MITZI		WINIFRED RENSHAW.
WILHELMINA		FIFI COOPER-EDMONDS
HEAD WAITER		VICTOR EVANS.
TONI (A Cabaret Star)		FIFI COOPER-EDMONDS.
FLUNKEY'S		⎰ FRANK EVANS. ⎱ FREDDIE BISIKER.

FLOWER GIRLS AND GUESTS.

L. Boughey	P. Laddiman	F. M. Rowlands
J. Corbett.	E. Lewis	K. Richards
P. Mason	J. Lloyd	G. Shelton
P. Dickinson	J. Mather	S. Teece
A. Dickson	M. Johnson	N. Westley
E. Fryer	W. Potts	M. Wellings

VIENNA DANCING TROUPE.

Peggy Dickinson, Margery Johnson, Ethel Lewis, Joyce Lloyd, Peggy Mason, Jose Mather, Kathleen Richards, Gladys Shelton.

SOLDIERS OF THE IMPERIAL GUARD AND WAITERS.

F. S. Estcourt	R. J. Humphries	C. S. Stevens
F. Evans	W. J. Martin	W. Sadler
S. I. Davies	E. H. Jones	E. Taylor
T. J. D. Grocott	M. Jones	V. Evans
J. Grant	T. Potter	J. G. Ward
H. Hawkins	E. B. Rowlands	

The Play Produced and Conducted by H. D. Westley.

Wellington Orchestral and Operatic Society switched allegiance from the Grand Theatre to the Clifton Cinema for their final production: *Good-Night Vienna!*, the cast of which appeared in the programme. The arrival of the Second World War in September 1939 saw an end to the Society and its highly polished and accomplished productions.

Celebratory programme cover commemorating the 1935-36 season when Wellington Town Football Club won the Birmingham and District League Challenge Cup and held the Shropshire Senior Cup.

Chapter Eight

Sporting Scene

In the old days, Wellingtonians always took their sporting activities seriously, whether they were staged in pubs, clubs or churches or on tables, walls, greens or pitches.

The weekly *Wellington Journal* gave detailed reports on matches, result charts and fixture details to ensure members of the public were kept up to date. With very little free entertainment available for those on restricted incomes, belonging to a sporting group became a vital (and healthy) pastime. Sporting habits generally began at school, where pupils had little choice but to take part. A competitive spirit in games was believed to contribute to the work ethic needed in later life. Perhaps it did.

Not everyone could be a 'first team' player. Identifying this photograph has been problematic but general concensus is that it is of the second or 'reserve' team of Wellington Town Football Club around 1938. Back row, from left to right: Dixon Davies, Bert Richards, Frank 'Danny' Williams, Frank Evans, Ernie Bates, Bob Black, -?-, Eric Adams, -?-, Frank Ellis?, Douglas Riley. Middle: Tom Foulkes, Joe Childs, Bob Latham, Ernie Austin, Frank Nagington, -?-, Arthur Jackson?, 'Honkey' Price. Front: -?-, Ken Saxon, G. Cross, -?-.

Wellington Town FC team, 1920-21, the season in which they won the Birmingham League, the Walker Cup, Shropshire Senior Cup and the Pearce Cup. Standing, from left to right: Mike Smith, Ebor Onions, Bill Thornton?, Billy Bowen?, Freddie Lloyd, George Hedgecox, Ernie Robinson, Murray Harris, Billy Littlewood, Bert Richards, Harry Rushton. Seated: Teddy Deakin, Joe White, Owen Steventon, Charlie Millington, Jack Churm, Ted White, Alf Sheldon, Len Capewell.

The band plays at the Buck's Head ground for the Shropshire Senior Cup final between Wellington Town and Shrewsbury Town on Good Friday, 1935. 11,836 spectators saw Shrewsbury win 2-1.

Report of an inter-school football match with Prince's Street school which appeared in a 1923 edition of the Constitution Hill school magazine.

School v. Prince's St.   Buck's Hd Grd.

This was the first encounter with our local rivals this season, and as their side had been strengthened by the inclusion of Geo. and Chas Millington (Sons of Mr C. Millington of W.T. F.C.) a good game was expected. Mr Alf. Riley kindly acted as Referee and Mr C. Millington ran the line.

There was little to choose between the Teams during the first quarter of an hour, but from this point the School, for a spell, had the better of the game, and E. Roden opened our score with a fairly easy goal from close range. This roused our opponents who quickly made tracks for Felton, and after heavy pressure during which the ball could not be scrambled away, Evason equalised with a shot that gave our goalie no chance. Just before half-time the visitors obtained the lead, Millington (G) beating several players and flashing a fast cross shot past Felton.

Half-time.— Prince's St. 2. School 1.

The School resumed with great determination, and were quickly on level terms through Tudor who finished a fine run with a brilliant goal. Keeping up the pressure the School gave the visitors' defence a trying time and King who was always pegging away, obtained the lead with a hard straight drive. The School had now assumed the upper hand and Tudor at outside left broke away time and again, to be at last rewarded with another goal. Close on time Lowndes reduced the lead with one of the best goals of the match, and F. Davies replied by increasing the School's lead to five. It was a very pleasant game. The School were a little superior in most departments, though Prince's St have the making of a splendid team. Result. School 5. Prince's St. 3.

Constitution Hill 'Excelsiors' football team, winners of the Wrekin Shield, 1927. Back row, from left to right: Percy Teece, Alf Johnson, Tommy Deakin, ? Robinson, Alf Whitcombe. Middle: 'Con' Hicks, 'Curly' Smallman, ? Hughes, ? Griffiths, Reg Green, ? Westwood. Front: Jack Pritchard, ? Westwood, Sid? Davies.

The Railway Shed Football Team of 1932, playing at the Buck's Head ground. Back row, from left to right: Ernie Dicken, Charlie Lewis, Walley Evans, -?-, -?-, -?-, Tom Pinches, -?-, Evan Roberts, -?-, Jack Pritchard, Bill Jones, Dick Batchelor (in trilby), -?-, -?-. Front: Jack Edwards, Joe Burdon, -?-, Bob Morgan, Hector Bradshaw, -?-, -?-.

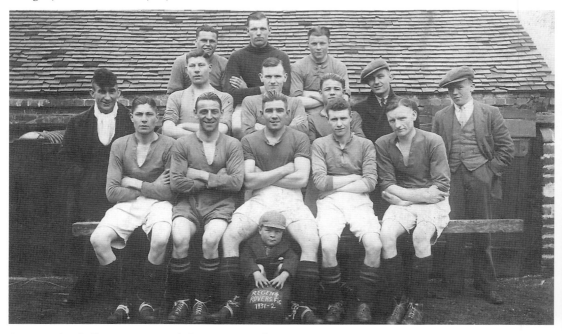

Amateur football teams attracted the attention of many youngsters wishing to display their prowess on the pitch. Several leagues sprang up to provide worthy opponents. Some teams represented public houses, whereas the 1931-32 Regent Rovers team may have been based in Regent Street.

Wrekin College (Wellington College until 1920) Rugby team, 1921. Included are I.M. Ashford, E.A. Bolton, H. Curtis, J. William Frost, R. Hall, D.W. Hawkins, C.F. Lettey, T.S. Leyshon, L.D. Narramore, Robert L. Neill, Kenneth W.H. Read, G. Rorton(?), C.G. Stanley, S.T. Stephenson and G. Wade.

Since its inception as Wellington College in 1880, Wrekin College has prided itself on encouraging sporting activities among its fee-paying students. Masters were also expected to become actively involved, as this 1920 team photograph shows.

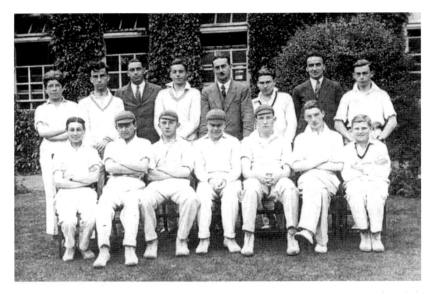

Wellington Boys' High school cricket team, 1932 or 1933. Back row, first left is Jeff Ball. Front row includes Ken Hayward (third from left) and Alf Grindley (second from right).

Cricket was not the sole province of the male population. Wellington Girls' High school shared buildings with the Boys' High school; perhaps they shared cricket bats as well. Girls were encouraged to try their hand at all manner of sports: this was the First (and probably only) XI in 1922.

Wellington Girls' High school, winners of the Shropshire County Netball Tournament, 1921. Back row, from left to right: E. Carter, M. Davis, M. Ward, I. Ward. Front: H. Smith, M. Whitehead, L. Davey.

Form IVa Hockey team at the Girls' High school, 1933. Back row, from left to right: C. Crewe, Miss Webster, E. Tunnock. Middle: N. Ward, P. Fletcher, G. Bailey, M. Shelly, A Pidgeon. Front: M. Piggot, N. Harris, S. Ricketts, G. Fish(er?).

Leading by example: tennis-playing staff at the Girls' High school, 1930. Back row, from left to right: M. Foster, A.B. Etches, ? Webster, D. Alcock, -?-. Front: I. Walker, D.A. Febling, N.S. Helm, ? Green, D.E. Geldart, N. Costling, A. Pickering Jones.

Wellington had a long tradition of sporting activities which attained widespread and enthusiastic support. Wrekin College played an active role in supporting amateur events and was happy to make its extensive and well maintained grounds available for community use.

Wellington Public Baths, opened in 1910 and providing slipper baths as well as this main swimming pool fed by water from Steeraway Reservoir, as it appeared around 1930. During winter months, the pool was drained for cleaning, covered with strong timbers and seating installed to enable theatrical productions, trade exhibitions and other 'dry' activities to take place.

Wrekin Road school won both boys' and girls' challenge cups at the 1922 Swimming Gala. Back row, from left to right: Miss F. Leeds, Mrs. L. Rogers, T. Warrall, G. Butter, A.E. Rogers, ? Jones, Cllr. Harvey. Middle: Annie Jones, Edna Simpson, Winnie Shelton, Alf Rogers, Albert Shenton, Olive Griffiths. Front: Fred Shelton, Richard Roberts, Billie Dolphin, Francis Shelton.

John Henry Twinney was just sixteen when this photograph of him with his championship trophies and medals was taken in 1925. The card on the table calls him Squadron Team Captain. His Royal Life Saving Society certificate was awarded in the same year.

Swimmer Phyllis Rogers, fifteen-year-old daughter of parents who were both Wellington Public Baths superintendents, won many awards for swimming and Life Saving. Seen here in 1928, she had just been awarded a certificate for teachers and instructors.

The YMCA in Wellington met in Wrekin Buildings on the corner of Tan Bank and Walker Street. The Association offered a wide range of activities, many of them of a sporting nature, including the Boys' Gymnastics Club, seen here in the summer of 1939.

Members of Wellington Boxing & Physical Culture School, 1932. Shropshire's leading welterweight boxer Billy 'Buller' Evans (born 1900) is second from the right in the middle row. He fought in public halls and fairground booths until the 1930s, his last bout won on points at the Orleton Fête in 1936.

Winners of the Wellington & District League in 1938 was the YMCA Table Tennis club. From left to right: L. Ward, E. Mosdell, F.D. Nye, C. Holmes and L. Stokes.

Shropshire Amateur Billiards Final in 1938 took place in the J. Lees' Tan Bank Billiards Hall. (Mr. T. Jordan's billiards hall in Cart Lane, later renamed Bank Road, closed in 1937). From left to right: C. Hickman (marker), J. Lees (referee), finalists J. Martin (Ellesmere) and L. Price (Oswestry) were finalists. Martin won, 500 to 290, his highest break being 91.

Waterloo Tennis Club in the 1920s met at Waterloo Road. Back row, second from the left is (James) William Davis and Ivor Machin is on the extreme right. Nora Smith (who married Ivor) sits fourth from the left while Gertie Bowles (who subsequently married William Davis) is second from the right.

Wellington Lawn Tennis Club members in the early 1930s. The club, which was situated along Church Walk off MIll Bank, had four grass courts.

Wellington Girls' High school first opened at Gospel Hall in New Hall Road in 1908 and moved to an impressive new King Street building in 1912. Girls were taught subjects essential to everyday life and office careers, like typing. The first headmistress, Miss E.B. Ross, was a progressive, encouraging academic and sporting achievement, some in the most unusual form. Even as late as the 1930s, deportment was classed as a physical activity, as was Table Laying: above participants await the judging of their napkins and place settings in the 1920s 'Tournament' above ... held in the gymnasium!

Members of Charlton Bowling Club, late 1920s, on the green outside their club house behind the Charlton Arms Hotel, Church Street. Many of its members were prominent businessmen.

SEVERN FISHERIES PROVISIONAL ORDER, 1911.

No. 1495

Year 1929.

SEVERN FISHERY DISTRICT.

LICENSE TO FISH WITH ROD AND LINE FOR FRESHWATER FISH.

(Not Transferable).

Not available after the 31st December, 1929.

Mr. *J H Swinney* of *Glebe St —* *Wellington* in the County of *Salop*

having paid the sum of TWO SHILLINGS for this License, is hereby authorised to fish for FRESHWATER FISH, with a single ROD and LINE, at the times and places at which he is otherwise entitled so to fish, within such part of the Severn Fishery District as lies within the watershed of the River Severn above Lincombe Weir, or within the watershed of the River Teme.

Given under the Seal of the Board of Conservators of the Severn Fishery District this 25 day of *May* 1929.

(Signed) **W. C. GERMAN,** Distributor.

FISHING TACKLE SPECIALIST.

IRONMONGER & SEEDSMAN,

WELLINGTON, SALOP.

The annual trout close season for rod and line in the Severn and tributaries above Borle Brook, Near Bridgnorth, and in the Teme and tributaries above Tenbury Wells Bridge is between the 15th September and 2nd March following, and in all other parts of the District between the 30th September and 2nd April following.

The open season for freshwater fish other than trout is from the 16th June to the 14th March following.

In the watershed of the River Severn below the point of confluence of the River Vyrnwy with the Severn other than the River Teme above Stanford Bridge the taking of Trout and grayling of a less size than 9 inches; bream, roach, dace, perch and chub of a less size than seven inches and gudgeon of a less size than four inches is prohibited and in the remainder of the District the taking of trout of a less size than seven inches is prohibited.

Trailing or trolling with natural or artificial spinning baits from boats in motion is prohibited.

Fishing was the most popular sport for men, but required a licence when angling in this district, which, during the interwar period, included reaches of the Rivers Severn and Avon, and Shropshire Union and Stroudwater Canals. Licences were purchased from pet shops or fishing tackle stores.

Wellington Golf Club members, late 1920s. The Club began as a nine hole course in 1905 and had expanded to 18 holes by 1909. By 1941 it was renamed Wrekin Golf Club.

Acknowledgements

Information included in this book has been obtained from a number of sources and contributors; where possible, every effort has been made to ensure factual accuracy. Apologies are made for the quality of some images, which have been included because of their rarity and the need to preserve as many of these socially and historically important illustrations as possible. Pictures, documents and supporting evidence have been supplied by the following, with further apologies to anyone or anybody that may have been inadvertently omitted.

Author's collection, G. Atkinson, G. Evans, R. Evans, *Hobson's Directories of Wellington*, *John Jones's Directories of Wellington*, J. Keay, *Kelly's Directories of Shropshire*, J. Lewis, J. Loach, P. Marston, J. Moore, P. Morris-Jones, T. Neal, New College, *Official Guides to Wellington, Salop, Shropshire Magazine, Shropshire Star*, I. Skelton, *Telford Journal*, D. Vickers, Wellington History Group, *Wellingtonia* magazine, *Wellington Journal & Shrewsbury News*, J. Whittingham and others who are no longer with us.

'General View of Wellington' – a *Princess Series* postcard from the 1920s. The photograph was taken from Ercall hill. The town cemetery lies in front of the gasholders on the left, while the bell tower and roof of All Saints parish church can be seen centre right.